STECK-VAUGHN

WORKFORCE: BUILDING SUCCESS

WRITING

Project Consultant

Harriet Diamond
Diamond Associates
Westfield, NJ

Series Reviewers

Nancy Arnold
Metropolitan Adult
Education Program
San Jose, CA

Lou Winn Burns
Booker High School
Sarasota, FL

Jane Westbrook
Weatherford ISD
Community Services
Weatherford, TX

Ronald D. Froman
National Training &
Development Specialists
Winter Springs, FL

Dr. Randy Whitfield
North Carolina Community
College System
Raleigh, NC

Ann Jackson
Orange County
Public Schools
Orlando, FL

STECK-VAUGHN
COMPANY
ELEMENTARY • SECONDARY • ADULT • LIBRARY

Acknowledgments

Steck-Vaughn Company
Executive Editor: Ellen Northcutt
Supervising Editor: Tim Collins
Senior Editor: Julie Higgins
Assistant Art Director: Richard Balsam
Design Manager: Danielle Szabo

Proof Positive/Farrowlyne Associates, Inc.
Program Editorial, Development, Design, and Production

Photo Credits
Cover Photo: © Superstock

ISBN: 0-8172-6522-8

Contents

To the Learner

Workforce: Building Success is a series designed to help you improve key job skills. You will find many ways to improve your skills, whether you're already working or are preparing to find a job. This book, *Writing,* is about writing to prepare for a job and writing on the job. You will need to fill out and create written documents to prepare for the workplace and also while you are on the job.

Before you begin the lessons, take the Check What You Know skills inventory, check your answers, and fill out the Preview Chart. There you will see which skills you already know and which you need to practice.

After you finish the last practice page, take the Check What You've Learned inventory, check your answers, and fill out the Review Chart. You'll see what great progress you've made.

Lessons include three types of exercises:

- The sentences in **Vocabulary Check** let you practice the new terms in context.
- The questions in **Comprehension Check** help you make sure you understood the lesson.
- In **Apply the Skill,** you will fill out forms and write letters using your personal information.

A Handbook is included in this book so you can review grammar skills. The section called **The Writing Process** will help you plan and edit your memos and letters.

At the end of the book, you will find a **Glossary** and an **Answer Key.** Use the Glossary to look up definitions of key work-related words. Use the Answer Key to check your answers to many of the exercises.

Check What You Know will help you know how well you understand writing skills. It will also show you which skills you need to improve.

Read each question. Circle the letter before the answer.

1. What should Jackie include in her resume about her education?

   a. her personal interests
   b. her goals
   c. areas of study and awards in high school and college

2. Oliver wants to get a full-time job in a bank. Oliver begins to write a list of people who would recommend him for a job. Oliver should list

   a. family members.
   b. friends.
   c. former teachers and employers.

3. Stanley interviewed for a job as a restaurant chef two days ago. Stanley should

   a. send a letter to thank the interviewer and express interest in the job.
   b. call the interviewer to talk about the job.
   c. wait to see if the interviewer calls him.

4. Dan uses a word processor to write his letters because

   a. he can rearrange words easily on the page.
   b. he doesn't have to worry about spelling.
   c. he can print many copies of the letter.

5. Joseph is going to send a form letter to ten people. To save time, he should

   a. type the addresses individually and copy the other information onto each letter.
   b. type each individual letter with the name, address, and information.
   c. write each letter by hand with the name, address, and information.

6. Ms. Gillaspy's assistant, Tom, receives a call and writes the date and phone number of the caller on a sheet of paper. What important piece of information is missing from this message?

    a. Tom's name
    b. the caller's name
    c. Ms. Gillaspy's phone number

7. Nancy's supervisor has asked her to write suggestions about how the company can increase its sales. Nancy could

    a. write a short letter.
    b. provide a list of pictures showing how sales could increase.
    c. write a report.

8. Sarah is an administrative assistant. She needs to inform 100 people that the parking lot will be repaved next week. She should write a

    a. memo to the staff.
    b. resume to the staff.
    c. customer service letter to the staff.

9. Bradley is filling out a job application. He does not have all the information with him to complete the form. He should

    a. leave some spaces blank and drop off the form.
    b. describe his situation to the employer.
    c. take the application home and fill it out completely with the required information.

10. On her first day of work, Tamara brings her Social Security card. She knows she will need it to

    a. show a picture ID.
    b. show her current address.
    c. complete insurance and tax forms.

11. Darnell is reviewing a coworker's work. He found her work to be excellent for the first six months, but incomplete for the last six months. Darnell should

    a. base his comments on the first six months only.

b. base his comments on the last six months only.

c. base his comments on the full year.

12. Tracey is preparing to write a letter to a customer about a refrigerator the customer bought. Tracey should include

a. facts about the refrigerator.

b. information about a different customer.

c. information about other products.

13. Sharon is preparing cover letters and business envelopes to mail to three employers. For each mailing, she should include

a. the employer's name on the letter only.

b. the employer's address on envelope only.

c. the employer's address on the letter and envelope.

Preview Chart

This chart will show you what skills you need to study. Reread each question you missed. Then look at the appropriate lesson of the book for help in understanding the correct answer.

Question Check the questions you missed.	Skill The exercise, like the book, focuses on the skills below.	Lesson Preview what you will learn in this book.
1. _____	Creating a resume	3
2. _____	Completing a personal data sheet	1
3. _____	Writing a follow-up letter	5
4. _____	Using a computer to write	7
5. _____	Using a computer to write form letters	11
6. _____	Writing phone messages	9
7. _____	Writing reports	13
8. _____	Writing a memo	8
9. _____	Completing a job application	2
10. _____	Completing tax and insurance forms	6
11. _____	Completing a performance appraisal	10
12. _____	Writing a customer service letter	12
13. _____	Preparing a cover letter and business envelope	4

Self-Inventory of Writing Skills

A. You have already developed some good writing habits. This self-inventory will help you find your strengths as a writer. It will also help you learn what you need to improve.

Circle the word at the right that best describes your habits. If a question doesn't apply to you, answer "sometimes."

1. When I fill out a form or application, I print neatly.   Always   Sometimes   Never

2. Once I finish writing a letter, I reread what I have written and make corrections.   Always   Sometimes   Never

3. I read the entire job application before filling it out.   Always   Sometimes   Never

4. I pay attention to punctuation.   Always   Sometimes   Never

5. I type or print when filling out a job application.   Always   Sometimes   Never

6. I read the instructions before I fill out an application for a bank account or a driver's license.   Always   Sometimes   Never

B. Use the chart below to find out how to rate yourself on the self-inventory.

	Number of Responses	Multiplier	Subtotal
Always	_____	× 3	_____
Sometimes	_____	× 2	_____
Never	_____	× 1	_____
		Your Total Score:	_____

SCORE

18–15 Very Good. You're well on your way to being a good writer.

14–9 Average. Your writing is good, but you need to practice.

8–6 Needs Improvement. Good try. Identifying problems with writing is the first step in solving them.

Lesson 1 Personal Data Sheet

A Personal Data Sheet

As you prepare to find a job, you need to ask yourself some questions. What kind of job experience do you have? What kind of work can you perform? These types of questions can be organized by a simple form or sheet. A personal data sheet is a form that includes important information about you and your skills. You can use a personal data sheet to complete a job application form and to create a resume. Here's a sample form to the right.

The following tips will help you complete your sample data sheet:

Objective: Think about the work you'd like to do. Write a brief statement about the kind of work you'd like to do.

Job Duties: State any special training you might have received on the job.

Skills/Other Experience: List any volunteer experience, such as helping out at a homeless shelter.

References: List people who can recommend you for employment. Former employers and teachers are best. Get permission before listing them.

Personal Data
Name: *Jamal Warner*
Address: *601 W. Tupelo*
City, State, ZIP Code: *Pleasantville, CA 99921*
Telephone: *(213) 555-5555*
Objective: *I am seeking an office job where I can use my computer skills.*

Work Experience
Company: *Elderberry Press*
Telephone: *(213) 555-6000*
Address: *2020 Melborne Road, Fairview Hills, CA 90001*
Dates of Employment: *9/15/90–9/27/92*
Job Duties: *Filing, telephone reception, word processing using Word Perfect, Word, and other programs*

Education
1990 Graduated Gull Lake High School, Richland, CA
1991 Attended Mill Valley Community College, Echo, CA

Skills/Other Experience (including volunteer experience)
I work very well with people and would like to have a job working with the public. I have strong telephone and computer skills. I also volunteer my time answering phones for a local social service agency.

References
Name: *Andrew G. Allen*
Title: *President*
Company: *Elderberry Press*
Address: *2020 Melborne Road, Fairview Hills, CA 90001*
Telephone: *(213) 555-6000*

Apply the Skill

Fill out this personal data sheet with information about yourself.

Personal Data

Name: _____

Address: _____

City, State, ZIP Code: _____

Telephone: _____

Objective: _____

_____

Work Experience

Company: _____

Telephone: _____

Address: _____

Dates of Employment: _____

Job Duties: _____

_____

Education

_____

_____

Skills/Other Experience (including volunteer experience)

_____

_____

References

Name: _____

Title: _____

Company: _____

Address: _____

Telephone: _____

Lesson 2 — Application Form

An Application Form

Every company has its own hiring policy, or way of hiring people. Many companies require you to fill out an application form. Others require a resume. Usually you fill out the form when you first apply for the job or at the time of your interview. An interview is a meeting with a possible employer. The purpose of the interview is to see if you are qualified for the job you are applying for. Some companies let you take the application form home. That way you can fill it out and mail it back. However, most companies require that you fill out the application form in person. Some employers use the application form instead of a resume. You can use your personal data sheet to help you fill out job applications (see Lesson 1).

Each time you fill out a job application, you have an opportunity to sell your skills and talents. The application form provides a lot of information about you in a small space. Employers use application forms to learn quickly about you.

Information on the Form

Although application forms may vary, most of them ask for the following:

- The date
- Your name
- Your Social Security number
- Your address and telephone number
- The type of job you are applying for
- Your skills and qualifications, or reasons that you are right for the job
- Whether you are over 18
- Education

- Past experience

- References, including telephone numbers

- Your signature (This authorizes or gives the company permission to investigate or check on the information on your application.)

Some application forms also ask for the following:

- Information on any physical limitations that would prevent you from doing the job

- Military service record, if any

- Hours you are available (can be there) to work

- Minimum salary (amount of money) you will accept

- Names of anyone you know who works for the company

- Whether you have applied to the company before

- Whether you have ever been convicted of a crime

- Whether you have a driver's license

- Whether you are qualified or licensed to operate any machinery

- Emergency notification name and phone number (This is the person you would like the company to call in case you are hurt or you become ill on the job.)

When you fill out an application form, you should either type or use a pen. Make sure that you read all the directions carefully. If the directions say to print your information, do not write it in cursive. If the form says to circle an answer, do not underline it. The application form is your first chance to show the employer that you can follow directions.

It's important to include all the information that is asked for. This is true even if you have to attach a resume that includes the same information. If a question doesn't apply to you, draw a line in the blank. That way the employer will know you didn't forget to fill it in.

A Sample Application Form

Read the following sample application form. Pay close attention to each item.

Read the application once before you fill in any of the blanks. This will help you answer the questions accurately.

Directions

Personal Data

APPLICATION FOR EMPLOYMENT

Complete all items. Print clearly with a pen. Sign the application.

Name: _Ruth Hubbard_
Social Security Number: _324-00-0000_
Address: _120 Holden Ave. Chicago, IL 60600_
Phone: _(312) 555-1245_

Employment Desired
Position: _Dental Assistant_
Date You Can Start: _July 15, 19XX_
Salary Desired: _$300/week_
Have you ever applied here before? (Check Yes or No.)
___ Yes ✓ No
Do you have any physical or mental condition that limits the type of work you can do? ___ Yes ✓ No
If yes, please explain. _____

Military Service
Have you ever served in the armed services of the United States?
___ Yes ✓ No
Have you ever been convicted of a crime? ___ Yes ✓ No
If yes, please explain. _____

Your Last School
Name: _Washington High School_
Address: _1400 West Lake Road, Halcyone, IL 60006_
From: _September 1987_ to _June 1991_
Did you complete? ✓ Yes ___ No

Employment History
Dates From/To: _12/18/91_ to _09/30/19XX_
Name and Address: _Shaw University Hospital, 12 Solley Road, Braiden, ME 04001_
Supervisor: _Alicia Mackey_
Position: _Dental Assistant_
Reason for Leaving: _Moved to Chicago_

I authorize the investigation of all statements contained in this application.
Date: _July 12, 19XX_
Signature: _Ruth Hubbard_

The directions ask for a check mark. You can assume that this direction applies to each Yes or No question on the form.

Some applications ask for your complete education, beginning with elementary school. This one asks only for your most recent education.

Most applications ask for your complete employment record, beginning with your most recent job.

An application is a written list of facts about you. It can help you persuade an employer that you would be a good person to hire. Honesty, accuracy, and neatness are qualities that employers appreciate in applications and in employees.

Vocabulary Check

Write the word that best completes each sentence. Choose from the list.

authorize   interview   notification   qualifications
available   investigate   policy   salary

Applications are used to find out about your _____

for a job. Each company has its own hiring _____ .

Most often you will fill out an application at the time of your

_____ . You fill in many different items, such as

the hours you are _____ to work and the minimum

_____ you would accept. In the emergency

_____ section, you write the name of the person

the company should call if you become ill or injured on the job.

By signing the application, you _____ the company

to _____ the information on your application.

Comprehension Check

Use Ruth Hubbard's application to answer these questions.

1. What kind of job is Ruth looking for? _____

2. How much money does Ruth want to make at her job?

   _____

3. Did Ruth attend college? _____

4. Where did Ruth work before? _____

5. Why did she leave her other job? _____

6. What does Ruth's signature at the bottom of the application

   mean? _____

   _____

Apply the Skill

Imagine that you are applying for a job in an office. Fill out the following application for the job.

APPLICATION FOR EMPLOYMENT

Complete all items. Print clearly with a pen. Sign the application.

Name: _____

Social Security Number: _____

Address: _____

Phone: _____

Employment Desired

Position: _____

Date You Can Start: _____

Salary Desired: _____

Have you ever applied here before? (Check Yes or No.)

___Yes ___No

Do you have any physical or mental condition that limits the type of work you

can do? ___ Yes ___ No

If yes, please explain. _____

Military Service

Have you ever served in the armed services of the United States?

___Yes ___No

Have you ever been convicted of a crime? ___Yes ___No

If yes, please explain. _____

Your Last School

Name: _____

Address: _____

From: _____ to _____

Did you complete? ___Yes ___No

Employment History

Dates From/To: _____ to _____

Name and Address: _____

_____

Supervisor: _____

Position: _____

Reason for Leaving: _____

I authorize the investigation of all statements contained in this application.

Date: _____

Signature: _____

Lesson 3 Resume

Your Resume

A **resume** is a written outline of your background or past experience. Employers use your resume to see if you are qualified for the job. Most resumes are one page long. Your resume should present the facts as an outline. An **outline** is a summary of the most important points about a subject. Your resume should use short groups of words. Refer to your personal data sheet (Lesson 1) to organize your resume.

There are many different ways to **format** or set up your resume. Most resumes contain the following main headings:

- Name, address, telephone number
- Objective
- Education
- Experience
- Skills

You may also want to include some optional information. This information is not required, but it might help an interviewer learn more about you. This section may include your interests, special skills, and talents. These facts may show your interviewer that you would make a good employee. You might list awards and honors you have received. You could explain your volunteer experience. Or you might list **references,** which are the names of people who like your work.

A resume is a sample of your work. Make sure it's done correctly. All the information on your resume should be up-to-date. It should be typed and should contain no errors.

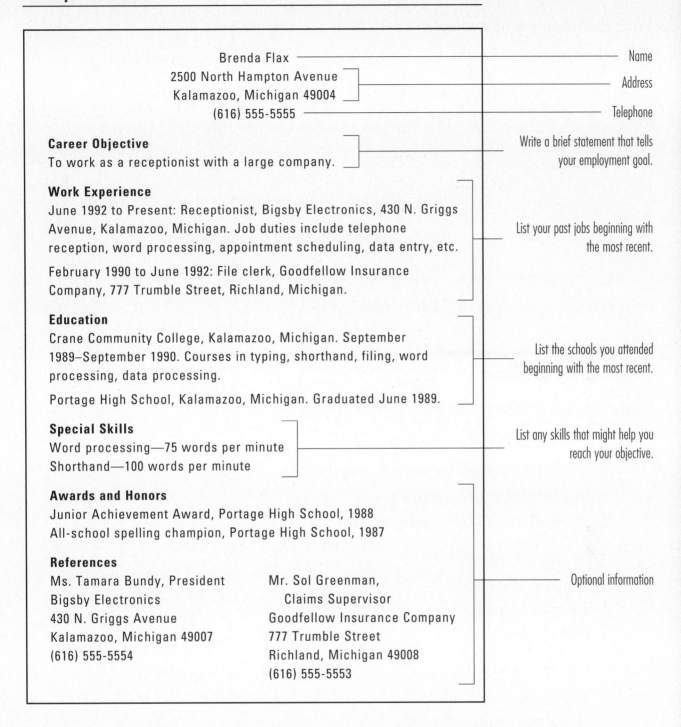

Brenda Flax — Name
2500 North Hampton Avenue
Kalamazoo, Michigan 49004 — Address
(616) 555-5555 — Telephone

Career Objective
To work as a receptionist with a large company.

Write a brief statement that tells your employment goal.

Work Experience
June 1992 to Present: Receptionist, Bigsby Electronics, 430 N. Griggs Avenue, Kalamazoo, Michigan. Job duties include telephone reception, word processing, appointment scheduling, data entry, etc.

February 1990 to June 1992: File clerk, Goodfellow Insurance Company, 777 Trumble Street, Richland, Michigan.

List your past jobs beginning with the most recent.

Education
Crane Community College, Kalamazoo, Michigan. September 1989–September 1990. Courses in typing, shorthand, filing, word processing, data processing.

Portage High School, Kalamazoo, Michigan. Graduated June 1989.

List the schools you attended beginning with the most recent.

Special Skills
Word processing—75 words per minute
Shorthand—100 words per minute

List any skills that might help you reach your objective.

Awards and Honors
Junior Achievement Award, Portage High School, 1988
All-school spelling champion, Portage High School, 1987

References
Ms. Tamara Bundy, President
Bigsby Electronics
430 N. Griggs Avenue
Kalamazoo, Michigan 49007
(616) 555-5554

Mr. Sol Greenman,
Claims Supervisor
Goodfellow Insurance Company
777 Trumble Street
Richland, Michigan 49008
(616) 555-5553

Optional information

Your resume is a list of facts that show a potential employer you qualify for the job you are applying for. Make sure your resume shows you off to your best advantage. You can do that by being neat and sticking to the facts.

Vocabulary Check

Write the word that best completes each sentence. Choose from the list.

background   format   outline   optional   qualified

A resume can tell a potential employer whether you are

_____ for the job. A resume contains facts about

your _____. There are many different ways to

_____ your resume. Most resumes are written in

_____ form. Some resumes may contain

_____ information that tells employers about your

interests, special skills, and talents.

Comprehension Check

Complete each sentence. Circle the letter in front of the answer.

1. Your resume is

   a. a written outline of your background.
   b. not important in an interview.
   c. a list of your likes and dislikes.

2. Your resume should be

   a. written in pencil.
   b. written in pen.
   c. typed.

3. A resume is usually

   a. one page long.
   b. two pages long.
   c. ten pages long.

Apply the Skill

Think of a job that you would like to have. Use a separate sheet of paper to create your own resume. Use the sample resume in this lesson as a guide.

Lesson 4

Cover Letter and Business Envelope

A Cover Letter

A cover letter is one kind of business letter. Business letters are more **formal** than the letters you may write to a friend or relative. The format of the letter should make it easy to read. The words should be clear and correct. All business letters have these five parts.

1. heading
2. inside address
3. greeting
4. body
5. closing

The purpose of a cover letter is to ask a company to consider hiring you. Send a cover letter with your resume. There are two reasons you might send a company a cover letter and resume:

- You might read the classified ads in the newspaper. An ad may ask you to send a resume with a cover letter.

- You might want a company to know that you are interested in working there.

The information you put in the body of a cover letter should do four things:

- State the specific job you are interested in.

- State how you learned of the job.

- Give your qualifications.

- Ask for an interview and say how the employer can contact you.

A cover letter should make a good first impression. Your cover letter lets the employer know why you are interested in the job. A letter that is neat and correct and gives information the employer needs also shows what kind of worker you are.

QUALIFIED OFFICE WORKER NEEDED. 45 wpm typing, general computer skills. Duties include typing, data entry, filing, and telephone answering. Hours M–F 8:00–5:00. Send a resume and letter to Anna Ross, New Century Manufacturers, P.O. Box 323, Los Angeles, CA 90042.

Suppose you find a newspaper ad for a job as an office worker, such as the ad on the left.

An applicant might send a cover letter such as the one below. Read the sample cover letter. Notice the five parts of a business letter. Also note what the letter says about the applicant's typing, filing, and general office skills. The letter shows that the applicant has the qualifications asked for in the ad.

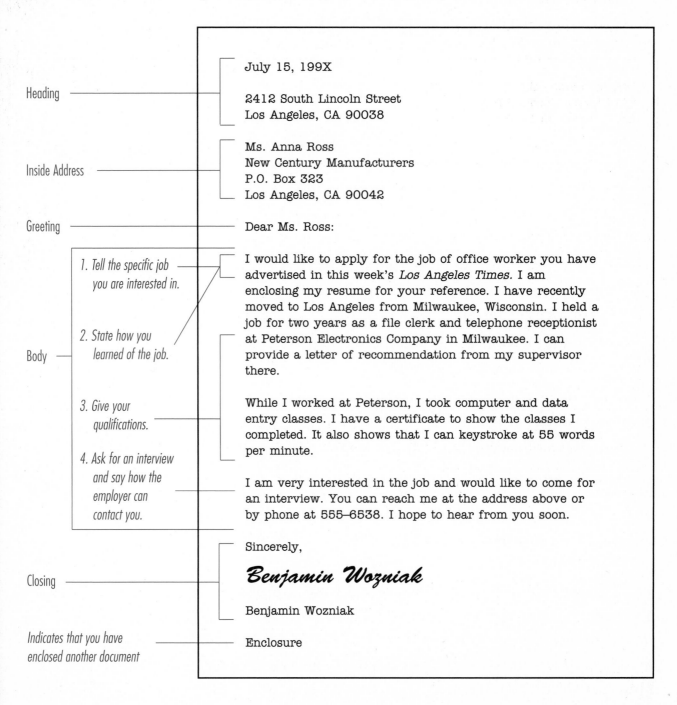

Heading

July 15, 199X

2412 South Lincoln Street
Los Angeles, CA 90038

Inside Address

Ms. Anna Ross
New Century Manufacturers
P.O. Box 323
Los Angeles, CA 90042

Greeting

Dear Ms. Ross:

Body

1. Tell the specific job you are interested in.

2. State how you learned of the job.

3. Give your qualifications.

4. Ask for an interview and say how the employer can contact you.

I would like to apply for the job of office worker you have advertised in this week's *Los Angeles Times.* I am enclosing my resume for your reference. I have recently moved to Los Angeles from Milwaukee, Wisconsin. I held a job for two years as a file clerk and telephone receptionist at Peterson Electronics Company in Milwaukee. I can provide a letter of recommendation from my supervisor there.

While I worked at Peterson, I took computer and data entry classes. I have a certificate to show the classes I completed. It also shows that I can keystroke at 55 words per minute.

I am very interested in the job and would like to come for an interview. You can reach me at the address above or by phone at 555–6538. I hope to hear from you soon.

Closing

Sincerely,

Benjamin Wozniak

Benjamin Wozniak

Indicates that you have enclosed another document

Enclosure

A Business Envelope

The envelope for your cover letter, or any business letter, has two parts:

- The address—the name, company, street or post office box, city, state, and ZIP code of the person to whom you are writing.

- The return address—your name, street or post office box, city, state, and ZIP code in the upper left corner.

Notice these two parts in the envelope below:

Benjamin Wozniak
2412 South Lincoln Street
Los Angeles, CA 90038

32¢

Ms. Anna Ross
New Century Manufacturers
P.O. Box 323
Los Angeles, CA 90042

A good cover letter explains why you are qualified for a certain job. It is meant to give a good first impression that will make the employer want to talk with you. A properly prepared envelope is the last step in making a good impression.

Vocabulary Check

Write the word that best completes each sentence. Choose from the list.

body   business   envelope   formal   greeting

A cover letter is a type of _____ letter. It is more

_____ than a letter to someone you know well.

The _____ of a cover letter includes all the

information you wish to tell someone. The _____

is a part of the letter that uses the name of the person to whom

you are writing. Your return address appears on the

_____ .

Comprehension Check

Use Benjamin Wozniak's letter to answer these questions.

1. What job is Benjamin applying for? _____

2. What is the name of the company that advertised the job?

   _____

3. What are his qualifications for the job? _____

   _____

4. What result does Benjamin want from his letter? _____

   _____

Apply the Skill

On a separate piece of paper, write a cover letter for a job you would like. You may want to look in the classified ads, or perhaps you have a job already in mind. Also address a business envelope.

A Follow-Up Letter

After you have had a job interview, it's a good idea to write a **follow-up letter** to the person who interviewed you. This is a kind of business letter. The main purpose of a follow-up letter is to show what kind of person you are. Possible employers will know from your letter that you are polite. They will see that you take initiative, that you follow through on things. A follow-up letter is not a formal application requirement. Writing a follow-up letter shows your interviewer that you are a person who does more than is required.

There are only a few things you need to include in a follow-up letter. These include:

- Thank the person who interviewed you.

- Note any materials that are enclosed with your letter. If the interviewer asked for more information from you, send it with your follow-up letter.

- Express enthusiasm, or excitement, about the job.

- Give the address and telephone number where you can be reached. The interviewer probably has that information already but he or she will be glad to have it close at hand.

- Say that you look forward to hearing from the company soon. This shows confidence without making you seem pushy.

A Sample Follow-Up Letter

After an interview, an applicant might send a follow-up letter like the one on the next page. Read the sample follow-up letter. Note the five parts of the business letter. Also look closely at the five parts of the body. These are the kinds of things you will want to include in your own follow-up letters.

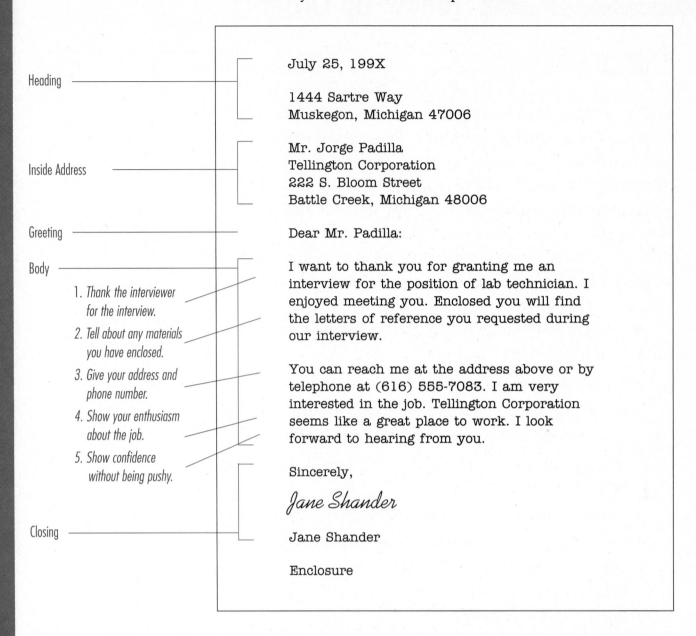

Heading
Inside Address
Greeting
Body

1. *Thank the interviewer for the interview.*
2. *Tell about any materials you have enclosed.*
3. *Give your address and phone number.*
4. *Show your enthusiasm about the job.*
5. *Show confidence without being pushy.*

Closing

July 25, 199X

1444 Sartre Way
Muskegon, Michigan 47006

Mr. Jorge Padilla
Tellington Corporation
222 S. Bloom Street
Battle Creek, Michigan 48006

Dear Mr. Padilla:

I want to thank you for granting me an interview for the position of lab technician. I enjoyed meeting you. Enclosed you will find the letters of reference you requested during our interview.

You can reach me at the address above or by telephone at (616) 555-7083. I am very interested in the job. Tellington Corporation seems like a great place to work. I look forward to hearing from you.

Sincerely,

Jane Shander

Jane Shander

Enclosure

It won't take you long to write a follow-up letter. After all, the interviewer already knows about you from your interview. Keep your letter short. Type it. Then **proofread** it, or check it for errors. Use the follow-up letter to put the final touches on your job interview.

Vocabulary Check

Write the word that best completes each sentence. Choose from the list.

enthusiasm   initiative   proofread
follow-up   interviewer

A _____ letter is a business letter you write to a

person who has interviewed you. It should thank your

_____ . Sending a follow-up letter also shows that

you take _____ . The possible employer will know

that you have _____ for the job. The last thing to

do before you send the follow-up letter is _____ it.

Comprehension Check

Use the information in the lesson to answer these questions.

1. What is the main purpose of writing a follow-up letter?

   _____

2. How does a follow-up letter show that you are polite?

   _____

3. How does a follow-up letter show that you take initiative?

   _____

   _____

4. Why might you enclose other items with your follow-up letter?

   _____

Apply the Skill

Imagine that you have just interviewed for a job at Homestyle Construction. You feel that your interview with Ms. Talitha Laine went well. You would really like to get this job. On separate paper, write a follow-up letter about your interview.

Lesson 6

Forms: W-4, I-9, and Medical Insurance

Forms

If you are hired, the first thing you will do at your new job is fill out three forms. One is a tax form called a W-4. Another is the Form I-9, or Employment Eligibility Verification. The I-9 shows employers that you are eligible, or authorized, to work in the United States. The third form is for medical insurance.

On your first day of work, you need to bring some personal documents to help you fill out the forms. Personal documents are printed materials that prove you are who you say you are. Bring as many of the following documents as you have:

- Social Security card or birth certificate
- Identification card. This can be a driver's license, state identification card, school identification with photo card, or military draft card.
- Up-to-date U.S. passport, certificate of U.S. citizenship, or foreign passport with employment authorization
- Social Security numbers for your spouse and children if you want them to be covered by your company's insurance plan

W-4

The purpose of the W-4 form is to supply information about you that your employer needs. The information on the W-4 form lets your employer know how much of your **income,** the money you make, to **withhold** or take out of your paycheck. The money is taken out for taxes. Your employer will pay the money toward your income taxes.

The W-4 form is fairly simple. You will fill in your name, address, and Social Security number. You also will need to give your marital status, which means to tell whether you are married or single. On line 4, you will tell how many allowances or dependents you are claiming. Dependents are those people who depend on your income. You can claim yourself, your spouse, and any children under the age of twenty-one. The more dependents you claim, the less money is taken out of your paycheck. If you are single and have no children, you can claim only one dependent, yourself.

A Sample W-4 Form

Joseph Balsam has just been hired at Blossom Hill Bakery. This is the W-4 he filled out.

Form **W-4** Department of the Treasury Internal Revenue Service	**Employee's Withholding Allowance Certificate** ▶ For Privacy Act and Paperwork Reduction Act Notice, see reverse.	QMB No. 1545-0010	

1 Type or print your first name and middle initial
Joseph   F

Last name
Balsam

2 Your social security number
366-00-0000 — Name and address
— Social Security number

Home address (number and street or rural route)
3221 Presley

City or town, state, and ZIP code
Hamtramck, Michigan 47220

3 Marital Status

☒ Single   ☐ Married
☐ Married, but withhold at higher Single rate.
Note: *If married, but legally separated, or spouse is a nonresident alien, check the Single box.*
— Marital status

4 Total number of allowances you are claiming (from line G above or from the Worksheets on back if they apply) . . . **4** *1* — Number of dependents
5 Additional amount, if any, you want deducted from each pay . . . . **5** $
6 I claim exemption from withholding and I certify that I meet ALL of the following conditions for exemption:
• Last year I had a right to a refund of ALL Federal income tax withheld because I had NO tax liability; AND
• This year I expect a refund of ALL Federal income tax withheld because I expect to have NO tax liability; AND
• This year if my income exceeds $550 and includes nonwage income, another person cannot claim me as a dependent.
If you meet all of the above conditions, enter the year effective and "EXEMPT" here . . . . ▶ **6** 19
7 Are you a full-time student? (Note: *Full-time students are not automatically exempt.*) . . . . **7** ☐ Yes ☒ No — Signature

Under penalties of perjury, I certify that I am entitled to the number of withholding allowances claimed on this certificate or entitled to claim exempt status.

Employee's signature ▶ *Joseph F. Balsam*   Date ▶ *7/24* .19 *9X* — Today's date

8 Employer's name and address (Employer: Complete 8 and 10 only if sending to IRS) | 9 Office Code (optional) | 10 Employer identification number

Leave items 8, 9, and 10 blank.

Form I-9

This form asks for your name, address, date of birth, and Social Security number. It also asks for your immigration status, which states the country where you are a citizen. You need to mark whether you are a U.S. citizen or a citizen of another country who has been authorized to work in the United States.

A Sample Form I-9

Read through the form below. Think about how you might answer the questions.

Last name first

Your last name or, if you have changed your name, the name you were born with

Immigration status

Sign your full name.

Today's date

EMPLOYMENT ELIGIBILITY VERIFICATION (Form I-9)

1. EMPLOYEE INFORMATION AND VERIFICATION: (To be completed and signed by employee.)

Name: (Print or Type) Last	First	Middle	Birth Name
Jackson	Darrel	J.	Jackson

Address: Street Name and Number	City	State	ZIP Code
1928 S. Dunleavy	Detroit	Michigan	43822

Date of Birth (Month / Day / Year)	Social Security Number
September 12, 1957	652-37-9436

I attest, under penalty of perjury, that I am (check a box):

☑ 1. A citizen or national of the United States.
☐ 2. An alien lawfully admitted for permanent residence (Alien Number A _____).
☐ 3. An alien authorized by the Immigration and Naturalization Service to work in the United States
　　 (Alien Number A _____ . or Admission Number _____ . expiration of
　　 employment authorization, if any _____).

I attest, under penalty of perjury, the documents that I have presented as evidence of identity and employment eligibility are genuine and relate to me. I am aware that federal law provides for imprisonment and/or fine for any false statements or use of false documents in connection with this certificate.

Signature	Date: (Month / Day / Year)
Darrel J. Jackson	October 5, 199X

Medical Insurance Form

Insurance covers your medical expenses in case you become ill or injured. If your company offers an insurance plan, a small part of each paycheck will go toward your insurance.

The purpose of a medical insurance form is to enroll or enter you into the company's insurance program. You may be asked to decide

- whether you want to use the company's health insurance plan.

- whether you want to enroll other family members in the insurance plan.

- whether you want dental insurance.

- whether you want the company's life insurance.

- who will be your beneficiary. This is the person who will receive payment from the life insurance company if you die.

- who the company should contact if you are involved in an emergency.

- whether you want to be on a disability insurance plan. Disability insurance provides money to support you and your family if you become unable to work because of illness or an accident.

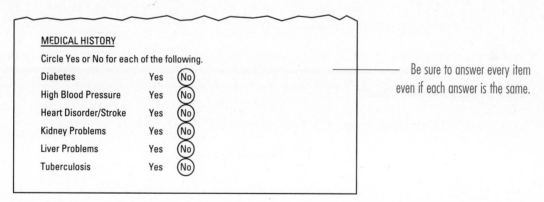

EMPLOYEE INSURANCE ENROLLMENT

Group Policy Number *1243901444* —————————— Provided by your employer

Employer Name ___ *Hendricks Pest Control* ___

Applicant Social Security Number ___ *374-00-0000* ___

Applicant Name ___ *Anna Crowley* ___

Single ___   Married *X*

Beneficiary Name ___ *Judson Crowley* ___ ———— The person who will receive benefits if you die

Relationship ___ *husband* ___

Employment Start Date ___ *12/02/XX* ___

COVERAGE INFORMATION

Medical ___   Employee only ___   Family *X*

Dental ___   Employee only ___   Family ___ ———— If you don't want the dental plan, put a line through the whole item.

Your insurance form will probably include a place for you to tell about any health problems you have. It usually includes a list of medical conditions. You will mark any illness or medical problem that applies to you.

MEDICAL HISTORY

Circle Yes or No for each of the following.

Diabetes   Yes   (No)
High Blood Pressure   Yes   (No)
Heart Disorder/Stroke Yes   (No)   ———— Be sure to answer every item even if each answer is the same.
Kidney Problems   Yes   (No)
Liver Problems   Yes   (No)
Tuberculosis   Yes   (No)

When you fill out any form, remember to

- read all the instructions.
- give all the information that is asked for.
- print neatly in pen or type.

Filling out tax, identification, and medical forms won't take very long. These forms are very important. Think of completing the forms as your first task at the new job.

Vocabulary Check

Write the word or term that best completes each sentence. Choose from the list.

beneficiary   disability   marital status
dependent   enroll   withhold

1. Your employer will _____ some money from

   each paycheck for taxes.

2. When you start an insurance plan, you _____

   in it.

3. A single person with no children can claim only one

   _____ .

4. Whether you are married or single is your

   _____ .

5. Your _____ is the person who will receive a

   payment from your life insurance company if you die.

6. _____ insurance is used when you are injured

   or sick and can't work.

Comprehension Check

Mark the following statements T (True) or F (False).

_____ 1. A W-4 is an insurance form.

_____ 2. You must name a beneficiary on your W-4.

_____ 3. Form I-9 is used for tax purposes.

_____ 4. You must give your immigration status on the Form I-9.

_____ 5. Most health insurance forms ask about your physical
condition.

_____ 6. You don't really need to read all the questions on an
insurance form.

Apply the Skill

Use the information from your own job or a job you would like to have to fill out the W-4 and the Form I-9 below.

Form **W-4** Department of the Treasury Internal Revenue Service	**Employee's Withholding Allowance Certificate** ▶ For Privacy Act and Paperwork Reduction Act Notice, see reverse.	QMB No. 1545-0010

1 Type or print your first name and middle initial	Last name	2 Your social security number

Home address (number and street or rural route) City or town, state, and ZIP code	3 Marital Status	☐ Single ☐ Married ☐ Married, but withhold at higher Single rate. Note: *If married, but legally separated, or spouse is a nonresident alien, check the Single box.*

4 Total number of allowances you are claiming (from line G above or from the Worksheets on back if they apply) . . . **4** _____

5 Additional amount, if any, you want deducted from each pay . . . . **5** $ _____

6 I claim exemption from withholding and I certify that I meet ALL of the following conditions for exemption:
- Last year I had a right to a refund of ALL Federal income tax withheld because I had NO tax liability; AND
- This year I expect a refund of ALL Federal income tax withheld because I expect to have NO tax liability; AND
- This year if my income exceeds $550 and includes nonwage income, another person cannot claim me as a dependent.

If you meet all of the above conditions, enter the year effective and "EXEMPT" here . . . . ▶ **6** 19 ____

7 Are you a full-time student? (Note: *Full-time students are not automatically exempt.*) . . . . **7** ☐ Yes ☐ No

Under penalties of perjury, I certify that I am entitled to the number of withholding allowances claimed on this certificate or entitled to claim exempt status.

Employee's signature ▶ _____ Date ▶ _____ .19

8 Employer's name and address (Employer: Complete 8 and 10 only if sending to IRS)	9 Office Code (optional)	10 Employer identification number

---

EMPLOYMENT ELIGIBILITY VERIFICATION (Form I-9)

1. EMPLOYEE INFORMATION AND VERIFICATION: (To be completed and signed by employee.)

Name: (Print or Type) Last	First	Middle	Birth Name
Address: Street Name and Number	City	State	ZIP Code

Date of Birth (Month / Day / Year)	Social Security Number

I attest, under penalty of perjury, that I am (check a box):

☐ 1. A citizen or national of the United States.

☐ 2. An alien lawfully admitted for permanent residence (Alien Number A _____).

☐ 3. An alien authorized by the Immigration and Naturalization Service to work in the United States (Alien Number A _____ . or Admission Number _____ . expiration of employment authorization, if any _____).

I attest, under penalty of perjury, the documents that I have presented as evidence of identity and employment eligibility are genuine and relate to me. I am aware that federal law provides for imprisonment and/or fine for any false statements or use of false documents in connection with this certificate.

Signature _____ Date: (Month / Day / Year) _____

Use your personal information to fill out this insurance form.

EMPLOYEE INSURANCE ENROLLMENT

Group Policy Number _____

Employer Name _____

Applicant Social Security Number _____

Applicant Name _____

Single ____   Married ____

Beneficiary Name _____

Relationship _____

Employment Start Date _____

COVERAGE INFORMATION

Medical ____   Employee only ____   Family ____

Dental ____   Employee only ____   Family ____

MEDICAL HISTORY

Circle Yes or No for each of the following.

Diabetes	Yes	No
High Blood Pressure	Yes	No
Heart Disorder/Stroke	Yes	No
Kidney Problems	Yes	No
Liver Problems	Yes	No
Tuberculosis	Yes	No

Lesson 7

Writing with a Computer

Computers and the Workplace

You will need to build your computer skills to prepare for the workplace. Computers will help you complete your work easily and quickly. You can use a computer to write a report, store information, and calculate figures. Letters, reports, and memos can be prepared using a computer. This lesson focuses on using a computer to write.

Basic Computer Functions

A **word processor** is a type of office machine. You will probably perform word-processing on a computer with a word-processing program. Word-processing programs let you do many things you would not be able to do on a typewriter. Some of the basic functions of a word-processing program include the following.

- **Input.** All word processors let you **input** your text by keystroking or typing on a keyboard. A computer keyboard is similar to a typewriter keyboard.

- **Move.** You can move words, paragraphs, or even whole pages to new positions in your document. Do this by using the cursor. Move text to rearrange topics in a letter or report.

- **Select.** A cursor is a flashing pointer that shows you where you are on the screen. Use the cursor to help you **select** or highlight text that you want to change.

- **Edit.** It is easy to make corrections when you're doing word processing. You can make **edits,** or changes and corrections, right on the screen. Edit to correct your grammar and sentence structure.

- **Print.** When all your corrections are finished, you can print out your text. This is called making a hard copy.

- **Delete.** You can **delete** or take out text at any time on a word processor. Use the cursor to highlight the text you want to take out. Then use the delete command, and the text disappears instantly.

- **Save.** All word processors have a **save** command. You save documents so that you can look at them again. If you do not finish your letter on Monday, you can save the part that you have finished. You may want to save onto a floppy disk to have an extra copy. This is called **backing up** your files.

More Advanced Functions

Word-processing programs have many functions and commands. Here are some more commands that will help you do your work.

- **Cut, Copy,** and **Paste.** These commands let you move or copy text from one document or file to another. If you are writing a letter to two people with the same information, you can copy the text from one letter and paste it onto a second letter.

- **Undo. Undo** lets you bring text back to the way it was if you make a mistake. If you accidentally delete text, use the undo command immediately. Your deleted text will reappear.

- **Search/Find/Replace.** The **search** or **find** command lets you find certain words in your text. The **replace** command lets you substitute one word or phrase for another.

- **Spelling Checker.** The computer has a built-in dictionary that can check spellings quickly. If it finds a misspelled word, it gives you the correct spelling.

Learn as much about computers as you can. The more you know about computers, the better your job skills will be.

Vocabulary Check

Write the word that best completes each sentence. Choose from the list.

delete   replace   spelling checker
hard copy   save   word processor
input   select

1. Many jobs require you to work on a computer or a

   _____ .

2. If you print out your text, you make a _____ .

3. When you get rid of text on your computer screen you

   _____ it.

4. Use the _____ command if you want to

   substitute one word or phrase for another.

5. If you think you have spelled a word incorrectly, you can use

   the _____ .

6. You can _____ your text by keystroking.

7. You use the cursor to help you _____ or

   highlight text that you want to change.

8. The _____ command lets you keep and look at

   text over and over again.

Comprehension Check

Complete each sentence. Circle the letter in front of the answer.

1. You can check your text for misspelled words by using the

   a. printer.
   b. spelling checker.
   c. undo command.

2. You can see where you are on the screen by using the

   a. window.
   b. cursor.
   c. spelling checker.

3. If you need to change a word that appears many times in a document, you

   a. save the document.
   b. create a hard copy by using the print command.
   c. use the search or find command to find and input the correction.

Apply the Skill

Complete one or both of these activities.

1. Find out where you can learn to use a word processor or improve your computer skills. You might check with your school, visit an adult education center or community college, or call the library. Are the classes free? When are classes scheduled?

2. Try to use a computer yourself. Check to see if your school has a computer lab. Try using the word-processing program. You might visit a public library, a copy shop that has computers, or a computer store. Input a few sentences and use commands to move, copy, and delete. Print an example of your work, if possible.

Lesson 8   Memos

A Memo

A memo is a form of internal communication. An **internal communication** is a way of sharing information inside a company. For example, one employee may send another employee a memo about an upcoming meeting. A supervisor may send a memo to his or her staff to announce company news.

A memo is most often used to share brief information. It might give employees new instructions or directions. A human resources department might send a memo about a new company **policy** or way of doing things. Employees use memos to provide short reports about projects and to update information. Memos are useful because they provide written records of conversations, meetings, or decisions.

A memo puts information into an easy-to-read format. The format uses four short headings at the top of the first page.

TO: (The person who is to receive the memo)
FROM: (The person who is sending the memo)
DATE: (The day on which the memo is sent)
SUBJECT: (What the memo is about)

The body of a memo can include the following:

• A summary of the information

• Details about the information

• A request for some kind of action

A Sample Memo

The memo below is from Abby Sinclair, who works in the human resources department. She is writing to Jane Hahn, who is heading the committee for the holiday party.

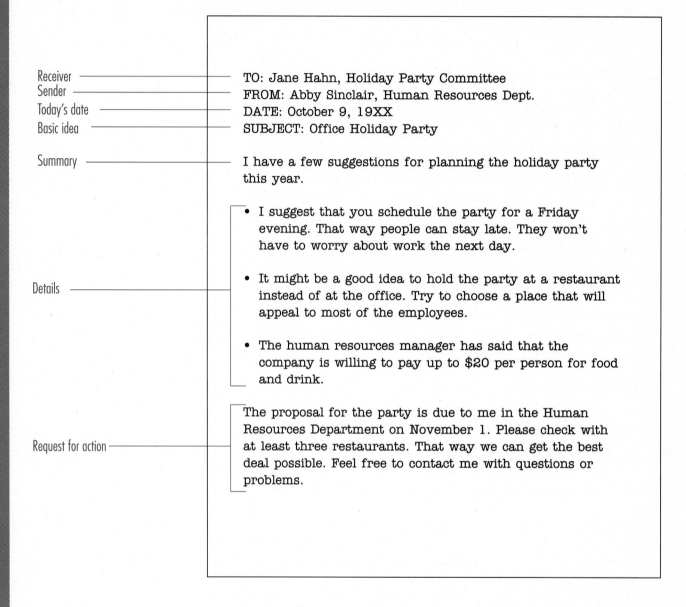

Receiver

Sender

Today's date

Basic idea

Summary

Details

Request for action

TO: Jane Hahn, Holiday Party Committee
FROM: Abby Sinclair, Human Resources Dept.
DATE: October 9, 19XX
SUBJECT: Office Holiday Party

I have a few suggestions for planning the holiday party this year.

- I suggest that you schedule the party for a Friday evening. That way people can stay late. They won't have to worry about work the next day.

- It might be a good idea to hold the party at a restaurant instead of at the office. Try to choose a place that will appeal to most of the employees.

- The human resources manager has said that the company is willing to pay up to $20 per person for food and drink.

The proposal for the party is due to me in the Human Resources Department on November 1. Please check with at least three restaurants. That way we can get the best deal possible. Feel free to contact me with questions or problems.

Notice how much information Abby put in this short memo. She could have met with Jane and talked things over with her. However, the memo saved her time. It also gives Jane a written record of Abby's suggestions and requests.

A memo is a form of communication that can save everyone time. Knowing how to write a memo will help you perform better on the job.

Vocabulary Check

Write the word or term that best completes each sentence. Choose from the list.

announcements   internal   summary
details   policy   update
instructions   request for action

A memo is an _____ communication. It is used to

make _____ or give _____ .

Sometimes a memo tells about a new _____ . It

might provide an _____ for old information. The

part that tells why the memo is being sent is the

_____ . The part of the memo that gives more

specifics is called the _____ . At the end of the

memo, there is often a _____ .

Comprehension Check

Mark the following statements T (True) or F (False).

_____ 1. Memos are more formal than business letters.

_____ 2. Internal communication takes place inside a company.

_____ 3. An update provides new information.

_____ 4. A policy is a request for action.

_____ 5. Memos are usually two or three pages long.

_____ 6. A memo can be a useful written record of a
conversation or meeting.

Apply the Skill

Imagine that you work in the Spring Valley Post Office. You want to meet with
the members of your department next week. You have an idea that will make
sorting the mail much easier. Write a memo to your department about the meeting.

E-mail and Phone Messages

Electronic mail (e-mail) and phone messages are used to send brief information. They help people communicate quickly. E-mail and phone messages often are saved only if a written record is required.

Phone Messages

When you take a phone message, always include this information:

- The name of the person the message is for
- The date and time of the call
- The name of the caller
- The phone number of the caller
- The message. Often the message is very short. It might be something like "Please call."

You might also include the caller's title, the caller's organization, and the times he or she can be reached.

Whenever you take a telephone message, remember to write neatly. Ask the caller to spell his or her last name unless you are already sure of the spelling.

Name of person to receive the message

Name of caller
Name of caller's organization
Caller's phone number with area code and extension

To _Ms. Entwhistle_
Date _9/15/9X_ Time _2:00 p.m._

WHILE YOU WERE OUT

M _Jo Cotter_
of _Helbig Plumbing_
Phone No. _(312) 555-0200 ext. 555_

TELEPHONED	X	PLEASE CALL	X
WAS IN TO SEE YOU		WILL CALL BACK	
WANTS TO SEE YOU		**URGENT**	
RETURNED YOUR CALL			

Message _Please call for plumbing estimate._

Operator _jtc_

A Sample Phone Message

Here is a phone message that a receptionist took for his boss.

E-mail Messages

An e-mail is a message sent from one computer to another. E-mail is formatted, or organized, to look a lot like a memo (see Lesson 8). You begin by creating a header on your screen. To **reply** to, or answer, an e-mail message, just hit the reply button while you are in the message you want to reply to. The header will be created for you. The header includes the following information:

- The To line for the e-mail name and address where the message is to be sent

- The Cc line for other e-mail names and addresses where you want your message sent

- The subject. This should be short but complete.

- The message you want to send

Remember to treat e-mail like any other piece of writing. E-mail is a document that can be saved and printed. Your coworkers depend on it to get information.

A Sample E-mail

The e-mail below was sent from Tanya Josta to Phillip Scutt at Highland Park.

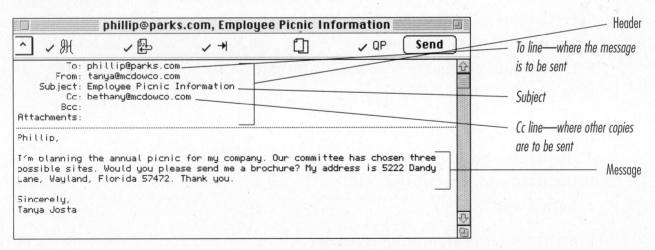

The ability to write good, accurate messages is an important job skill. Make sure that you pay careful attention when you send and receive e-mail and phone messages.

Vocabulary Check

Write the word that best completes each sentence. Choose from the list.

e-mail
formatted
header
reply
transmit

Sending messages can be done through your computer

using _____. This type of message is

_____ like a memo. It is a simple process to

send or _____ e-mail. At the top of your e-mail

message is the _____ . If you want to answer or

_____ to an e-mail, your header will be created

for you.

Comprehension Check

Complete each sentence. Circle the letter in front of the answer.

1. E-mail and phone messages are used

   a. to communicate quickly.
   b. to communicate large pieces of information.
   c. in place of business letters.

2. Phone messages should always contain

   a. the name and phone number of the caller.
   b. the date and time of the call.
   c. both a and b.

3. E-mail messages should be written

   a. when you already know the person.
   b. in a format like a memo.
   c. when you don't expect an answer.

Apply the Skill

1. Fill out the message to the right:

   Mr. Bell called Ms. Adkins at 4:15 on the afternoon of July 5. Mr. Bell's area code is (414). His telephone number is 555-5252. His extension is 1057. Mr. Bell works for Bell's Business Warehouse. He wants Ms. Adkins to call him. He is returning her call. He wants to schedule a sales call.

   ```
   To _____
   Date _____ Time _____

        WHILE YOU WERE OUT

   M _____
   of _____
   Phone No. _____
   ┌─────────────────────┬────────────────────┐
   │ TELEPHONED          │ PLEASE CALL        │
   ├─────────────────────┼────────────────────┤
   │ WAS IN TO SEE YOU   │ WILL CALL BACK     │
   ├─────────────────────┼────────────────────┤
   │ WANTS TO SEE YOU    │                    │
   ├─────────────────────┤ URGENT             │
   │ RETURNED YOUR CALL  │                    │
   └─────────────────────┴────────────────────┘
   Message _____
   _____
   _____
   _____
   _____
                Operator _____
   ```

2. Now fill in the blank e-mail screen below. Imagine that you are writing to Abdul Shuring at Everett Clothing. His e-mail address is shuring@everett.aol.com. You are writing about a shipment of bathing suits that has not arrived at your store. You have received a bill from Abdul for the whole shipment. Tell him that you have not received the swimsuits. You also want to send a copy of your e-mail to his supervisor at the e-mail address jenny@everett.aol.com.

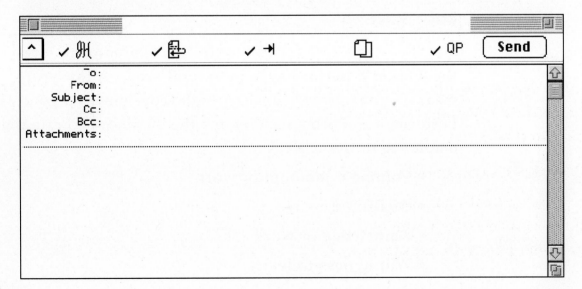

Performance Appraisal

A Performance Appraisal

A performance appraisal is an evaluation, a way of judging your work. Every company has its own policy about performance appraisals. At most companies, your supervisor will evaluate your work once a year. Sometimes your performance is reviewed after your first 90 days on the job. Some companies ask employees to evaluate themselves, their coworkers, and their supervisors.

Companies usually evaluate their employees for three reasons:

- To make note of how well an employee works

- To point out areas for the employee to improve

- To make decisions about pay raises

Performance appraisal forms often have two parts. The first part is fill-in-the-blank. The second part is a rating, or grading, sheet. Sometimes the appraisal includes the job title and duties of the employee. In most companies, both the employer and the employee must sign the form.

Rating Scales

Most appraisal forms require the evaluator to **rate** the worker's performance in several areas. A low score means a poor performance. A high score means a good performance. Forms usually ask the evaluator to rate the employee in these areas:

- Volume or amount of work

- Quality of work

- Knowledge of work

- Willingness to learn

- Ability to work with others
- Ability to take initiative or do more than is required

Some companies also rate employees on:

- Punctuality or being on time

- Customer service

- Appearance

The overall rating is the average of all scores. For example, suppose you were evaluating an employee using a rating scale of 1 to 5. If the employee received four 3s and four 4s, he or she would receive an overall rating of 3.5.

When you fill out an appraisal, you need to remember a few things. First, be accurate and fair. Don't exaggerate or go beyond the truth about the person's strong or weak points.

Second, base your evaluation on the whole work period that is being evaluated. For example, if an employee has been working for six months, don't evaluate only his or her first two weeks of employment. Evaluate performance based on the entire six months.

Third, avoid using double standards. A double standard happens when you judge one employee by different rules than you use for others. Evaluate each person using the same rules to be fair to everyone.

Fourth, keep performance appraisals **confidential.** These evaluations are private. You shouldn't discuss an appraisal with anyone but the employee you are evaluating or a supervisor.

PERFORMANCE EVALUATION	Strictly Confidential

Last Name	First Name	Middle Initial
Cho,	Mark	S.

Date employee was hired — Employment Date _9/02/9X_   Appraisal Date _9/15/9X_

Date of performance appraisal — Reason for Review _annual review_   Date of Last Review _9/12/9X_

Time period being appraised — Period of Report _one year_   From _9/13/9X_   To _9/15/9X_

Job Title _cook_   Current $ _15.00_ wk. (hr.)

Employee's salary — Date of Last Increase _9/12/9X_   Amount of Increase _$2.00/hr._

Date of last pay raise

Amount of last pay raise

Attendance Records During Review Period

sick days used _0_   personal days used _2_   times late _0_

vacation days used _6_   vacation days remaining _4_

RATING SCALE
1 = Performance is well below expected levels
2 = Performance is acceptable, but production is below expected levels
3 = Performance is consistently within expected levels
4 = Performance consistently exceeds expected levels
5 = Performance consistently exceeds superior levels

Rating scale —

EMPLOYEES ARE TO BE APPRAISED ON THESE FACTORS

	1	2	3	4	5
volume of work					✓
quality of work					✓
knowledge of work					✓
ability to learn new duties			✓		
effective communication			✓		
organizing own work					✓
initiative					✓
attitude and cooperation		✓			
ability to get along with others		✓			
appearance					✓

Average of all appraisal scores — **OVERALL PERFORMANCE RATING (Circle one) 1 2 3 (4) 5**

Both signatures required —

Elvin Marcos _9/15/9X_	_Mark Cho_ _9/15/9X_
Reviewer's Signature/Date	Employee's Signature/Date

A performance appraisal tells employees how well they are doing. You can use a performance evaluation to help you improve your skills. Concentrate on those areas that need some improvement. As your job skills improve, so will your performance appraisals.

Vocabulary Check

Write the word that best completes each sentence. Choose from the list.

confidential   initiative
evaluation   volume

1. A performance appraisal is an _____ of an

   employee's work.

2. How much work an employee does is his or her

   _____ of work.

3. When you do more than is asked for, you are taking

   _____ .

4. Performance appraisals are kept private because they are

   _____ .

Comprehension Check

Use Mark Cho's performance appraisal to answer the following questions.

1. How long has it been since Mark's last performance appraisal?

   _____

2. How many days was Mark absent during the period of this

   performance appraisal? _____

3. How much money did Mark make per hour during the

   performance period before this one? _____

4. In what two areas of his job does Mark need the most

   improvement? _____

5. What does Mark Cho's overall performance appraisal mean?

   _____

   _____

Apply the Skill

Fill out the performance appraisal using this information:

Rene Jenks is a file clerk who has worked with you for six months. He is often late for work. His work is often incomplete. Sometimes his handwritten reports are not readable. He gets along very well with others. He always does what he's told, but he never does anything on his own. He makes $10 an hour.

PERFORMANCE EVALUATION

Strictly Confidential

Last Name   First Name   Middle Initial

_____

Employment Date _____   Appraisal Date _____

Reason for Review _____   Date of Last Review _____

Period of Report _____   From _____ To _____

Job Title _____   Current $ _____ wk. / hr.

Date of Last Increase _____   Amount of Increase _____

Attendance Records During Review Period

sick days used _____   personal days used _____   times late _____

vacation days used _____   vacation days remaining _____

RATING SCALE
1 = Performance is well below expected levels
2 = Performance is acceptable, but production is below expected levels
3 = Performance is consistently within expected levels
4 = Performance consistently exceeds expected levels
5 = Performance consistently exceeds superior levels

EMPLOYEES ARE TO BE APPRAISED ON THESE FACTORS

	1	2	3	4	5
volume of work					
quality of work					
knowledge of work					
ability to learn new duties					
effective communication					
organizing own work					
initiative					
attitude and cooperation					
ability to get along with others					
appearance					

OVERALL PERFORMANCE RATING (Circle one) 1 2 3 4 5

_____   _____
Reviewer's Signature/Date   Employee's Signature/Date

Form Letters

A Form Letter

A form letter is a letter used to communicate the same information to a large number of people. It includes some general information for everyone and some specific information that changes from person to person. You might write a form letter to all your customers to tell them about new store hours. Using form letters can save you time.

A form letter is made up of two kinds of computer files. One is a database file and the other is a word-processing file. To create a personalized form letter, you **merge** or join together the two files.

A Database File

When you send a form letter, some of its information changes from person to person. This information makes up the **database file.** The database file has several items. Look at the sample database file to understand the different parts. The top row of information is the header. The header tells what kind of information is in each column. Information is input, or typed, into the computer into blocks or **fields** of type. Each small piece of information has its own field. The computer commands you use will depend on what type of computer program you're working on. You will need to create separate fields for each of the following:

- Title (Mr. or Ms.), first name, last name
- Company
- Street address
- City
- State
- ZIP code

A Sample Database File

Look at the sample database file below. Note the six fields for information that changes from letter to letter.

The header contains the names of all the fields.

Each row contains one complete data record.

Each field contains one kind of information.

If a record does not have information for one of the fields, leave it blank.

Name	Company	Address	City	State	ZIP Code
Mr. Evan Blake	Blake Heating	522 W. Bank St.	Hamburg	IL	60717
Ms. Harriet Childs		21 S. Central Ave.	Kenilworth	IL	60719
Ms. Shawn Barker	The Right Stuff	P.O. Box 56001	Augusta	MI	46003

A Sample Word-Processing File

The word-processing file contains the information that will be the same for each person receiving the form letter. This information is called **boilerplate.** When you create the boilerplate, leave placeholders for the information you will merge from the database file. The placeholders are for the date, names, company names, addresses, and greetings. In the example below, note which parts are boilerplate and which are placeholders.

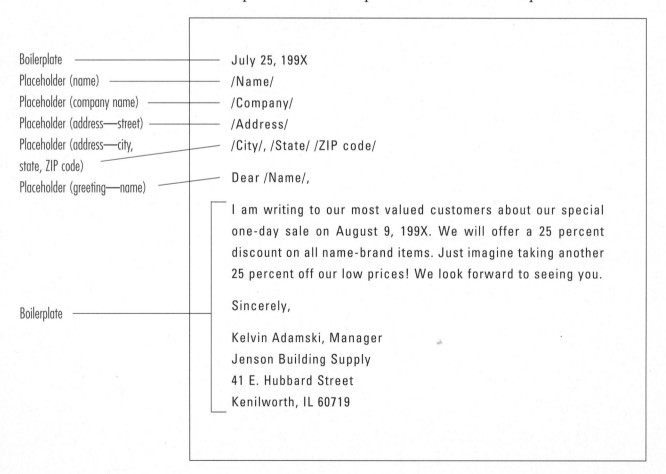

Boilerplate ——————— July 25, 199X

Placeholder (name) ——————— /Name/

Placeholder (company name) ——————— /Company/

Placeholder (address—street) ——————— /Address/

Placeholder (address—city, state, ZIP code) ——————— /City/, /State/ /ZIP code/

Placeholder (greeting—name) ——————— Dear /Name/,

I am writing to our most valued customers about our special one-day sale on August 9, 199X. We will offer a 25 percent discount on all name-brand items. Just imagine taking another 25 percent off our low prices! We look forward to seeing you.

Sincerely,

Boilerplate ———————

Kelvin Adamski, Manager
Jenson Building Supply
41 E. Hubbard Street
Kenilworth, IL 60719

When you merge your database file with your word-processing file, you will have a form letter for each name in the database. Each person will get the same basic letter. But each letter will have the person's own name and address.

Word-processing programs vary, so you may learn several ways to create a form letter. If your company doesn't have a database program, you can still create personalized form letters. All you have to do is write the boilerplate text. Then use the computer save as command to rename each letter. Insert the address for each letter after you rename it.

Vocabulary Check

Write the word that best completes each sentence. Choose from the list.

boilerplate   database   header   merge

1. To create a form letter, you _____ two different

    kinds of files.

2. A _____ file contains the information that is

    different for each person receiving the form letter.

3. Information that is the same for each person receiving the form

    letter is called _____ .

4. The part of the database file that names the different fields is

    called the _____ .

Comprehension Check

Use information in the lesson to answer these questions.

1. What are the two kinds of computer files you use to make a

    form letter? _____

2. What does merging these two files do? _____

    _____

3. What is the purpose of a form letter? _____

4. What are three things that might make up fields in a database

    file? _____

Apply the Skill

Visit a library to use their computers. Create a form letter that merges database
information with a word-processing file. Create a database of at least three
names and addresses where you want your form letter to go.

Lesson 12 Customer Service Letters

Customer service letters are letters sent from a company to its customers. These letters should be brief, polite, and professional. Choose your words carefully so the customer knows you are interested in serving him or her.

There are many reasons for sending a customer service letter. Some of those reasons include:

- To request information from the customer
- To request an action, such as paying a bill or filling out a form
- To respond to a customer's inquiry or question
- To tell a customer about his or her **order** or purchase
- To respond to a customer complaint
- To offer or give useful information to the customer

Format

A customer service letter is a business letter. It looks similar to a cover letter, which you wrote in Lesson 4.

The body states your reason for sending the letter. It gives details and provides all the information your customer might need. Be sure that all your information in the letter is correct and up-to-date. The body also resolves, or takes care of, the issue stated in the letter. Resolving the issue might mean that you request or ask for action from the customer. It might mean that you tell the customer about something the company plans to do. For example, a company may announce a plan to open a new store or have a sale.

A Sample Customer Service Letter

Read the following customer service letter. It is an answer to a customer complaint.

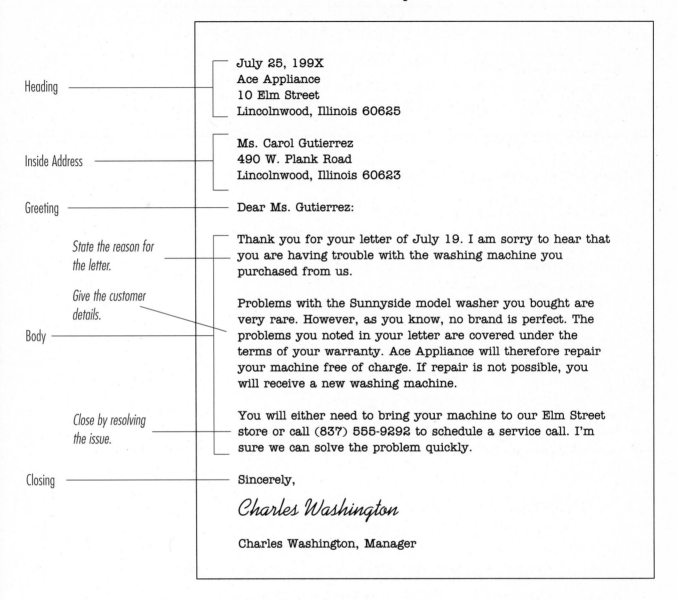

Heading

July 25, 199X
Ace Appliance
10 Elm Street
Lincolnwood, Illinois 60625

Inside Address

Ms. Carol Gutierrez
490 W. Plank Road
Lincolnwood, Illinois 60623

Greeting

Dear Ms. Gutierrez:

State the reason for the letter.

Thank you for your letter of July 19. I am sorry to hear that you are having trouble with the washing machine you purchased from us.

Give the customer details.

Body

Problems with the Sunnyside model washer you bought are very rare. However, as you know, no brand is perfect. The problems you noted in your letter are covered under the terms of your warranty. Ace Appliance will therefore repair your machine free of charge. If repair is not possible, you will receive a new washing machine.

Close by resolving the issue.

You will either need to bring your machine to our Elm Street store or call (837) 555-9292 to schedule a service call. I'm sure we can solve the problem quickly.

Closing

Sincerely,

Charles Washington

Charles Washington, Manager

Notice that Charles Washington stated his reason for sending the letter. He gave his customer some details about the situation. Then he resolved the issue.

In your job, you may or may not have to deal with customer complaints. Knowing how to write a customer service letter is a job skill that will help you in almost any job.

Vocabulary Check

Write the word that best completes each sentence. Choose from the list.

complaint   inquiry   request   resolve

1. When a customer asks a question, he or she makes an

   _____ .

2. A customer who is unhappy with something a company did is

   likely to make a _____ .

3. When you ask a customer to do something, you

   _____ an action.

4. The last part of the body of a customer service letter should

   _____ an issue.

Comprehension Check

Mark the following statements T (True) or F (False).

_____ 1. All customer service letters deal with complaints.

_____ 2. The body of a customer service letter should complain
to the customer.

_____ 3. The main purpose of a customer service letter is to
resolve an issue.

_____ 4. Customer service letters should always be polite.

_____ 5. Customer service letters look like cover and follow-up
letters.

_____ 6. Customer service letters only include the header.

Apply the Skill

Use a separate sheet of paper to write a customer service letter. Imagine you
work for Sports Court, a sporting goods store. A customer named Ann Trio
wrote you a letter on February 6, 199X. She asked when the Lader tennis racquet
would be available. Tell her that the racquet will be in the store in March.

Reports

A Report

The purpose of a report is to provide information. This information often comes from research. **Research** includes anything you have studied carefully. Your research might include information you learn from books or meetings.

Businesses often use reports to help them make decisions. The information in a report should be complete and clear. It should be in a readable, or easy-to-read, format. For example, you might be asked to write a report that answers a production problem or a customer's question. Or you might write a report on a specific **topic** or subject.

There are several different kinds of reports. An internal report is one that is sent within the company. A **progress report** gives information about the status of a project. It may tell whether the project is on schedule and on budget. Progress reports are updated weekly or monthly to tell what has been done and what work remains. Or you might write a report to **recommend,** or suggest, a procedure for organizing office supplies. Reports provide information and may suggest improvements for a company or a department.

Collect Information

Where do you get the information to write a report? Following are two tips to help you collect information:

- **Conduct a survey.** A **survey** is a list of questions about a subject. For example, suppose your supervisor asks you to restock the department supply area. You need information about what supplies your department needs. You might prepare a list of questions for the people in your department. A sample question might be, "Do you use drafting paper?" The answers to your survey would tell you what supplies your department needs. You could then write a report about your findings.

- **Use resources.** Visit a library to gather research. Most libraries have their resources listed on a computer catalog. Use the computer catalog to locate newspaper or magazine articles about the subject of your report. Find books on your topic. Ask a librarian for help. For example, suppose you work in a restaurant and need information about companies that make a special type of cooking oil. You can find this information in a library and use it to prepare a report.

Report Format

To get started, ask yourself "Why am I writing this report?" The answer will help you organize your ideas. Also, think about who will read your report. What information would be helpful to them? A report starts with a short statement about the topic or the reason for writing the report. Next, your report should present the facts about your topic. Put your facts in a **sequence** or order. One of the most common ways to present the facts is in chronological order. **Chronological** means the order in which events happened. Some other ways to present facts are to arrange them by subject or by order of importance.

Once you have presented the facts, write a conclusion. A **conclusion** summarizes the facts. Your conclusion might include your recommendations about how to solve a problem. A conclusion can also ask for input from others about how best to solve a problem.

A Sample Report

Read the following progress report that Anne Ayala wrote for her boss.

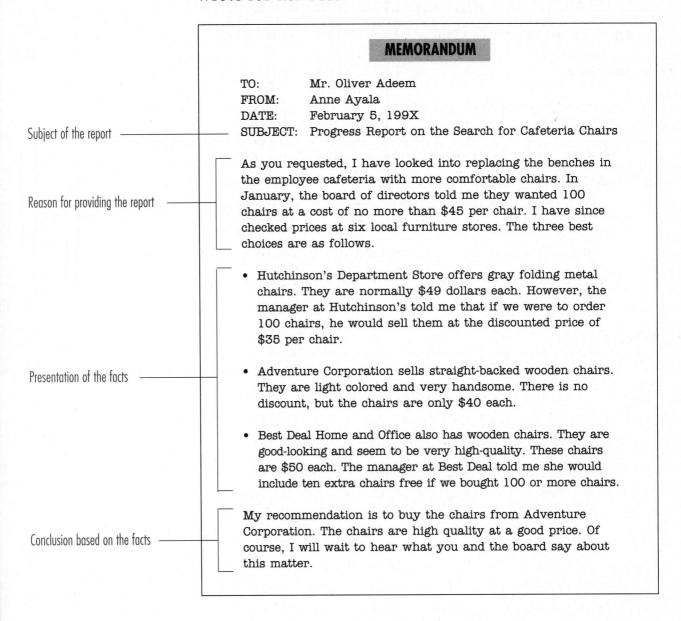

Subject of the report

Reason for providing the report

Presentation of the facts

Conclusion based on the facts

MEMORANDUM

TO: Mr. Oliver Adeem
FROM: Anne Ayala
DATE: February 5, 199X
SUBJECT: Progress Report on the Search for Cafeteria Chairs

As you requested, I have looked into replacing the benches in the employee cafeteria with more comfortable chairs. In January, the board of directors told me they wanted 100 chairs at a cost of no more than $45 per chair. I have since checked prices at six local furniture stores. The three best choices are as follows.

- Hutchinson's Department Store offers gray folding metal chairs. They are normally $49 dollars each. However, the manager at Hutchinson's told me that if we were to order 100 chairs, he would sell them at the discounted price of $35 per chair.

- Adventure Corporation sells straight-backed wooden chairs. They are light colored and very handsome. There is no discount, but the chairs are only $40 each.

- Best Deal Home and Office also has wooden chairs. They are good-looking and seem to be very high-quality. These chairs are $50 each. The manager at Best Deal told me she would include ten extra chairs free if we bought 100 or more chairs.

My recommendation is to buy the chairs from Adventure Corporation. The chairs are high quality at a good price. Of course, I will wait to hear what you and the board say about this matter.

Always keep a copy of any report you create. Later, you can go back to it if you need to review or revise it.

You may be asked to write reports for many different situations. Writing clear, complete reports is an important job skill. Reports can help you and your coworkers and bosses make decisions.

Vocabulary Check

Write the word or term that best completes each sentence. Choose from the list.

conclusion   progress   survey   research   topic

In a report, you present information that you have gathered

through _____ . You might be asked to write a

report on a specific _____ . You might write a

_____ report to tell the status of the schedule.

To gather information from coworkers, you might prepare a

_____ or list of questions. A report's

_____ is based on the facts presented in the

report.

Comprehension Check

Complete each sentence. Circle the letter in front of the answer.

1. A report usually starts with

   a. the reason for writing the report.
   b. the conclusion based on the facts.
   c. a presentation of the facts.

2. A sequence that tells the facts in the order in which they happened is

   a. subject sequence.
   b. chronological order.
   c. order of importance.

Apply the Skill

Write a rough draft of a short report. Make your report two or more paragraphs. You might write a report about how your classmates feel about a situation, service, or product. Or write a progress report about what you've done at work or in class during the last week. Use correct report format.

Handbook

The Handbook gives you more instruction and practice with grammar skills. Writing on the job is important to your success. The material in this Handbook will help you make sure your writing is correct. The last part of this Handbook tells you how to plan and organize your writing. If you need more practice with a certain skill, you can refer to the appropriate page in this Handbook.

Handbook Contents

When should you begin a word with a capital letter? A capital letter marks the beginning of a sentence. Names of people and important places and objects are also capitalized. Different rules apply for each kind of word and word group. The following rules will help you decide when to capitalize a word.

- Capitalize the first word of every sentence.

  Most offices have fax machines.

- Capitalize names of people and titles before names.

  Dr. Lena Kasten   **Ms. Suszek**
  Governor Lincoln

- Capitalize the names of companies, buildings, institutions, and streets.

  Ford Motor Company   **Trump Tower**   **Mercy Hospital**
  Madison Avenue

- Capitalize the names of continents, countries, states, cities, towns, mountains, rivers, and other bodies of water.

  Asia   **Mexico**   **Arizona**   **Mount Hood**   **Lake Mead**

- Capitalize days, months, historical events, and holidays.

  Monday   **May**   **World War I**   **Thanksgiving**

A. Rewrite the following sentences with correct capitalization.

1. on monday, ursula lawson applied for a job as a junior assistant to mayor Blake.

_____

_____

2. she drove down haynes road to get to mayor blake's office in the price building.

_____

_____

3. one of the mayor's assistants, mr. crawford, asked ursula to fill out an application.

_____

_____

4. on the application, ursula was asked if she was a citizen of the united states.

_____

_____

5. ursula filled out the application on monday, july 1, 1997.

_____

_____

B. The last question on the application was, "Why do you want a job with the mayor's office?" Ursula's answer is below. Circle the words that need capitalization.

by working with the mayor, I hope to have a positive effect on the city of cleveland. from april of 1990 until january of this year, I worked for senator cass in sacramento, california. one of my jobs was answering questions about the california state government. I also taught government classes at the university of northern california. I enjoyed my job and would like to continue doing similar work here in ohio.

Punctuation

Punctuation marks such as periods and question marks give readers important information. They tell you when a sentence ends. They tell you if a sentence is a question or a statement. Following are some rules for the punctuation marks that are used most often in writing on the job.

Two punctuation marks are used to end sentences.

- A **period** ends a statement.

    Go past the elevators and turn left.

- A **question mark** ends a question.

    Which direction is Deon's office?

Punctuation appears inside a sentence, too. Commas, colons, and apostrophes are all forms of punctuation.

- A **comma** is used to tell a reader when to pause in a sentence.

    Even though Shawn wanted to call the client herself, she didn't have time.

- A comma is also used to separate items in a list or within dates, numbers, titles, and addresses.

    May 10, 1952 $5,200   Lupe Diorio, M.D.   Miami, FL

- A **colon** is used to show that a list or an example follows.

    Naomi needed a few supplies: a stapler, a hole-punch, and ten envelopes.

- A colon is also used after a greeting in a business letter, between numbers when telling time, and to set off a conclusion or summary.

    Dear Ms. Kehoe: 4:00 P.M.

    He opened the office door and found none of his coworkers inside: it was a holiday.

- An **apostrophe** is used to show missing letters in a **contraction**. *I'm* is a contraction. The apostrophe takes the place of the missing *a*.

It is becomes **it's.**
Who is becomes **who's.**
She is becomes **she's.**
What is becomes **what's.**

- An apostrophe is also used to indicate possession or ownership. A possessive is formed by adding *'s* (for nouns that don't end in *s*) and *'* (for nouns that end in *s*).

  I think you have Dewayne's pens.
  He left it in the employees' conference room.

Exercises

A. Mark each sentence with a period or a question mark.

1. Which computer program will create graphs
2. There are many different graphing programs
3. Which program you choose depends on what kind of graphs your company needs

B. Add commas to the sentences below.

1. Lydia learned that her raise would take effect on June 1 1998.
2. Karen found out that it would cost $1100 to repair the computers in the finance office.
3. Jake's Body Shop is in South Bend Indiana.

C. Add colons to the paragraph below.

Maura has many reasons to look for a new job. She wants full-time work from 900 A.M. to 500 P.M., a shorter commute, and a salary increase. Her choices include the following working at a temporary agency, working at her sister's office, working at her son's school, and working at her husband's office.

D. Insert apostrophes as needed in the following items.

1. Johnathans tax form
2. Dont use the fax machine. Its broken.
3. She shouldnt call.
4. Shes worked since 1990.
5. on Torys desk
6. Its his mothers idea.
7. Whos in charge?
8. Whats this?

Run-ons and Sentence Fragments

Two common errors in sentence structure are run-on sentences and sentence fragments.

A **run-on** sentence is two or more sentences that are written together without correct punctuation.

Susan's job revolved around communication with other departments she did nothing else.

Independent clauses are complete thoughts that can stand alone as sentences if punctuated properly.

Susan's job revolved around communication with other departments. She did nothing else.

A **sentence fragment** is a group of words that does not fully state a complete thought. It is often missing a subject or a verb or both. The subject of a sentence is the word that a sentence is about. Be careful when you use words such as *although*, *if*, and *because*. Sentence fragments often begin with these words.

If Josephine's work is complete.

The reader does not know what will happen if Josephine's work is complete. This is a sentence fragment. To fix a fragment, join the fragment to another sentence, or make sure it has a subject and a verb.

If Josephine's work is complete, she will start a new task.

Exercises

A. Read the run-on sentences below. Add the correct punctuation to the following sentences.

1. James, the human resources manager, hired a qualified person to fill the entry-level accounting position she had experience in accounting.

2. Her resume listed three previous jobs she held in finance she worked for Electricus for the past eight years.

3. Shawn was repairing the engine the customer called to ask when he could pick up his car.

4. Shelly opened the flower shop early in the morning for her suppliers they often arrived before 7:30.

B. Mark the following items F (Fragment) or C (Complete Sentence).

_____ 1. If Stefan decides to apply for a promotion in his company.

_____ 2. Even though Ms. Barrett has decided to promote Stefan's coworker Gina.

_____ 3. When Gina learned she was promoted, she smiled.

_____ 4. Although a formal process has not been established yet.

_____ 5. We listened to the presentation.

_____ 6. Because Brad listened to his customer.

Nouns

A **noun** names a person, place, idea, or thing. *Job, manager, office,* and *decision* are all nouns.

- To make most nouns **plural,** add *-s.* When a word ends with *s, sh, ch, x,* or *z,* add *-es* to make the plural form.

  book + s   **choice + s**   **lake + s**   **glass + es**

- Some plural nouns are irregular. The following are examples of irregular plural nouns.

Singular	Plural
child	children
man	men
person	people
tooth	teeth
woman	women

Pronouns are words used in place of nouns. Here is a chart of personal pronouns. The words in the middle column are possessive pronouns. They can be subjects or objects of the verb.

Personal Pronouns

Subject Pronouns	Possessive Pronouns	Object Pronouns
I	mine	me
you	yours	you
he, she, it	his, her, its	him, her, it
we	ours	us
you	yours	you
they	theirs	them

A pronoun must agree in number with the noun it refers to.

Incorrect: John left for the meeting. **They** will be back this afternoon.

Correct: John left for the meeting. **He** will be back this afternoon.

Exercises

A. Write the plural form of each noun.

1. speech _____

2. class _____

3. business _____

4. disk _____

5. course _____

6. bus _____

7. address _____

8. tax _____

B. Circle the nouns and pronouns in the sentences.

1. Maricela calculated the balance. Then she faxed it to the bank.

2. At the end of the day, the police officer filled out the arrest reports. He gave them to his assistant.

3. Sharon organized the receipts for the day. Then she counted the cash in her register.

C. Circle the correct pronoun in each pair of sentences.

1. The kitchen workers like the new piece of equipment. (It, He) chops vegetables quickly.

2. The flight attendants are ready to leave. (She, They) have the tickets.

3. Sam gave the reports to Kristin. (They, It) were printed and copied.

Verbs

A **verb** is a word that expresses action or being. Read the example.

Dolores goes to work early on Tuesdays.

The verb in the sentence is *goes.* It tells the reader what Dolores does on Tuesdays. Every sentence must have a verb. The **tense** of a verb shows time of action. It lets a reader know when an action takes place. The three simple tenses of verbs are present, past, and future.

Present	Past	Future
write	wrote	will write

A **regular verb** forms its past tense by adding *-d* or *-ed*. If a verb ends in *-y,* change the *y* to *i* and add *-ed*.

arrive   arrived   order   ordered   copy   copied

An **irregular verb** doesn't have an *-ed* past tense form. Irregular verbs change form in various ways. Read the examples of irregular verbs.

Present	Past	Present	Past
am, is, are	was, were	do	did
begin	began	eat	ate
break	broke	ride	rode
come	came	tell	told

If you are unsure of the spelling of an irregular verb, check a dictionary.

Subject-verb agreement means that the subject and verb of a sentence match or agree.

- A singular subject takes a singular verb.

  Mitch is ordering grass seed for the golf course.

- A plural subject takes a plural verb.

  All the roofing companies were busy after last month's big storm.

Exercises

A. Complete the chart of verb forms below.

Present	Past	Future
work		
		will understand
	thought	
have		
		will apply
	went	
know		
	called	
send		

B. Change the underlined verb to the past tense.

1. The plumber <u>check</u> all the pipes for leaks. _____

2. Sarah <u>use</u> the computer to find the information. _____

3. The crew <u>do</u> most of their work before it <u>begin</u> to rain. _____ _____

4. Diana <u>tell</u> us about the new health plan. _____

C. Complete each sentence using the correct form of the verb in parentheses.

1. (to organize) The court reporter _____ the reports tomorrow.

2. (to push) The nurse's aide _____ the cart into the operating room an hour ago.

3. (to drive) Stella and Sam _____ to the station when it rains.

Modifiers

A **modifier** is a word or phrase that describes other words or phrases. An **adverb** modifies a verb, an adjective, or another adverb. Adverbs tell where, when, and how. The word *quickly* is an adverb.

Adjectives modify nouns and pronouns. They help the reader picture the nouns by telling which one, how many, how much, or what kind. In the phrase *gray machine,* the adjective is the word *gray. Gray* describes the machine. The following are examples of modifiers.

Adjective	Adverb
quick	quickly
easy	easily
hard	hard
good	well

To change a sentence with adjectives to a sentence with adverbs, you need to rewrite the sentence.

Jordan is a <u>good</u> cook.

He cooks <u>well</u>.

When using modifiers, keep them close to the words they describe. A **misplaced modifier** is placed too far from the word or phrase that it modifies. This can confuse the reader. The following is an example of a misplaced modifier.

Salespeople often need to use telephones <u>with pagers</u>.

In this sentence, it is unclear if the telephones have pagers or if the salespeople have pagers. The underlined phrase needs to move closer to the word it is modifying.

Salespeople with pagers often need to use telephones.

In writing, you want to make your message as clear as possible. If you use adjectives and adverbs correctly, your readers will understand what you mean.

Exercises

A. Circle the modifier that fits best in each sentence below.

1. The equipment in the new bicycle factory was not working (good / well).

2. Ralph, the manager, said the chances are (good / well) that the machines will be fixed today.

3. The butcher cut the meat (quick, quickly) but (careful, carefully).

4. (Slow, Slowly) the tired firefighters walked out of the building.

5. Janie thinks it is (easy, easily) to arrange flowers (beautiful, beautifully).

B. If needed, rewrite each sentence below, placing the modifier in the correct position. Some sentences may not need correcting.

1. In the blender, the chef mixed the ingredients for the filling.

_____

2. Driving in the fog, the bus driver could not see the traffic.

_____

3. The painter began work on the house wearing overalls.

_____

4. By scheduling meetings in the evenings, the new project can be completed by the department leaders.

_____

5. Tasha chose to meet with her supervisor early in the morning instead of in the afternoon.

_____

6. She said something about the finance department's report walking from her office to the meeting.

_____

7. Containing over fifty software disks, Jennifer was cleaning out the file cabinet.

_____

Spelling

To write well, you need to spell well, too. Some words are difficult to spell. However, there are rules that can help you spell many words. This lesson contains tips that will help you spell correctly.

Spelling Rules

There are rules for spelling words when you add endings to the words. These rules apply to endings that start with a **vowel,** such as the endings *-ing, -ed, -er,* and *-est.*

- For most words, just add the ending.

  answer   +   -ed   =   answered
  remind   +   -er   =   reminder

- If a word ends in *e,* drop the *e* and then add the ending.

  take   +   -ing   =   taking
  nice   +   -er   =   nicer

- If a one-syllable word ends in a **consonant** with a vowel before it, double the last letter and add the ending.

  cut   +   -ing   =   cutting
  big   +   -est   =   biggest

- Another spelling rule that is frequently used is this: Put *i* before *e* except after *c,* or when sounded like *a* as in *neighbor* and *weigh.* It's best just to memorize this rule. Below is a list of some examples of this rule.

  believe   friend   piece   receive   weight

There are some exceptions to the *i* before *e* rule. You need to memorize how to spell the words below since they are exceptions.

either   height   neither   science   their

Using the Dictionary and Spelling Programs

Since all spelling rules have exceptions, a dictionary is a writer's most important tool. When you write, look up any words whose spelling you are not sure about.

Usually, different forms of a word, such as the present and past tenses of a verb, are listed together. Irregular forms are also listed separately. For example, to find out how to spell the past tense of *pay*, you can look up *pay* or *paid*. Here is what a dictionary will tell you.

paid \pād\ *past of* pay.

pay \pā\ **paid, paying** to give money or goods in return for work or other goods.

If you are working on a computer, you may have a spelling program that checks the spellings of words. The program points out words that are misspelled. Some programs offer suggestions for the correct spelling.

Homonyms

Homonyms are words that sound alike but have different meanings and spellings. These words can cause readers confusion if not used correctly. Spelling programs will not catch a word that is spelled correctly but used incorrectly. Read the following example.

Incorrect: Who's book is this?
Correct: Whose book is this?

A spelling program will not find the mistake in the first sentence since *who's* is a contraction for *who is.* This is a usage mistake. Don't rely on a computer to catch all your mistakes. Check your work carefully for mistakes like this one.

The following is a list of some common homonyms.

aloud	allowed	right	write	rite
hear	here	there	they're	their
he'll	heal	too	two	to
higher	hire	way	weigh	
I'll	aisle	weight	wait	
it's	its	we're	were	
know	no	we've	weave	
one	won	who's	whose	
piece	peace	you're	your	
red	read			

Exercises

A. Circle the correct homonyms in the paragraph below.

Luke Cinders is setting up a display (for, four) the K-Tech trade show. He is putting (to, too, two) engines over (hear, here) where everyone can (sea, see) them clearly. He needs to put each (piece, peace) in the (right, write) place.

B. Add the endings *-ed* and *-ing* to the following words.

1. stop   _____   _____
2. name   _____   _____
3. work   _____   _____
4. time   _____   _____
5. phone   _____   _____
6. wrap   _____   _____
7. input   _____   _____
8. order   _____   _____
9. hire   _____   _____

C. Circle the correct word to complete each sentence.

1. Is it true that (your/you're) using a spelling checker?
2. (I'll/Aisle) watch you so I can learn how to use it, too.
3. (Here's/Hears) the computer manual if you want to read it.
4. I found a lot of useful tips for word processing in (they're/there).
5. (It's/Its) time for all of us to practice word processing.
6. (We're/Were) learning more about how to improve our writing.
7. I met someone (who's/whose) an expert computer technician.
8. (He'll/Heal) provide the disk with the file.
9. (We've/Weave) asked the supervisor for more training.
10. I can't (weight/wait) to start the training class.

D. Circle the misspelled word in each sentence and write it correctly.

1. My freind started working at my company last month. _____

2. Niether of us had seen her at lunch. _____

3. She'll be takeing courses that help her keep up with her job. _____

4. Did you recieve your first paycheck yet? _____

5. After working here a year, I beleive it's a good company. _____

6. This year I received the bigest pay raise I ever made. _____

7. Now I'm the assistent to the head of our department. _____

8. The mail room will check on the wieght of these letters. _____

9. Handling letters and packages is thier main job. _____

10. By Febuary I'll have my own car. _____

11. I apreciate working here and getting a regular paycheck. _____

12. An assembler's pay is based on the number of peices he or she makes. _____

13. I've been saveing money to buy a car. _____

14. The hospital is paying for her sceince courses. _____

The Writing Process

The writing process is a four-step way to help you write effectively. The four steps include gathering and organizing your ideas, writing, checking your writing, and revising your writing.

Gathering and Organizing Ideas

Planning helps a writer decide what to say by gathering and organizing ideas. Follow these tips for gathering ideas.

Choose Your Topic. The topic is the subject you write about. It's the main message you want to give your readers. Choosing one topic keeps your writing clear and to the point. All your other ideas will relate to this topic.

Decide Your Purpose. Your purpose is a clear statement that tells your readers your reason for writing. Your purpose might be to explain or complain.

Take Notes. Finally, think about what you would like to say and write your ideas. Your notes don't need to be complete sentences. Read these notes for a memo Tiffany Clark will write about a meeting.

time of meeting
place of meeting
let staff know about training schedule for new computer system
date of meeting
explain why new system will help everyone be more efficient
tell everyone that the company is doing great this year

Notice that she tried to write all the ideas she wants to talk about in the memo.

After gathering ideas, organize them using these tips:

Group Your Ideas. Look at your notes, and put similar ideas into the same group.

Choose Your Ideas. Look closely at your ideas. Some ideas may not be as good as others. Are all the ideas about your topic? Cross off any that are off the topic. Do some ideas repeat information? Cross off these ideas.

Put Your Groups in Order. Review your topic and purpose. Think about what information your readers will want to know first. How can you arrange your ideas clearly? You might organize ideas in time order or by order of importance. Number the groups in the order you think is best.

Usually, you do not need to rewrite your list when you organize. Just use circles, lines, and numbers to indicate groups and order. Here is how Tiffany Clark organized the information for her memo about the meeting.

Notice that the writer grouped time, date, and place together. Note, too, that she crossed out the idea about the company doing well. This idea is not about the topic. She numbered her groups from 1 to 3 to show the order she will use when she writes the memo.

Exercises

A. Read the steps for gathering and organizing ideas. Number the steps in order from 1 to 6.

_____ Group your ideas.

_____ Decide your purpose.

_____ Take notes.

_____ Put your groups in order.

_____ Choose your ideas.

_____ Choose your topic.

B. Roy wants to apply for an after-school job as a clerk at a sporting goods store. He made the following list of ideas to put in a cover letter to go with his application. Group Roy's ideas, choose the ones he should use, and put them in order.

the job I'm applying for

I played in the band

I have two brothers and a sister

when I'm available for an interview

I get along well with people

I play several sports and know a lot about sporting goods

I found the job listing on the Internet

C. Your department is having a meeting next week to discuss the new sick leave and vacation policies. Your boss asked you to write a memo telling everyone about the meeting. First, gather information on a separate piece of paper. Then, organize the information.

Writing

After you have planned and organized your ideas, you are ready to write. You know what you want to say and how you want to present your ideas. Now, you need to build on what you have already done. The writing stage includes three steps.

Write the Introduction. The **introduction** is your beginning. It usually tells your readers what your topic and purpose are. Your introduction can be fairly short.

Write the Body. The **body** is the main part of your document. In the body, you develop and explain your ideas. The body is usually the longest part of your document.

Write the Conclusion. The conclusion is the last part of your document. Writers often summarize, or briefly review, their topic and purpose in the conclusion. The conclusion will probably be about as long as the introduction.

When you write, do not worry if you make a mistake. You will have a chance to correct your writing in the next step. Read the memo Tiffany Clark wrote about computer training.

MEMORANDUM

TO: Order Processing Department
FROM: Tiffany Clark
SUBJECT: Computer Training
DATE: July 21, 199x

The department will begin using the new computer system in about two weeks.

In order to help everyone learn the new system, two training sessions have been scheduled. Here are the times, dates, and locations of the sessions:

Tuesday, July 27   2 to 4 P.M.
Thursday, July 29   9 to 11 A.M.

The new computer system offers several advantages over the old one. It will let us enter orders more quickly. It will also let us tell customers whether their orders are in stock.

I look forward too seeing you at the training sessions.

Exercises

A. Match the words with the definitions. Write the letter of the correct answer.

_____ **1.** introduction   a. You explain your ideas in this part of your document.

_____ **2.** body   b. You briefly review information in the body in this part of the document.

_____ **3.** conclusion   c. You tell the reader your topic in this part of your document.

B. Bob, the owner of a print shop, wrote the following notice about emergency planning to his employees. The parts of the notice are out of order. Fix it by putting 1 next to the introduction, 2 next to the body, and 3 next to the conclusion.

EMPLOYEE NOTICE

_____ When you hear the weather siren, remain calm. If you are on the phone, tell the caller you will call back as soon as possible. If you are working at a computer, save your work and shut down your computer. If you are working on the large machines in the back, turn them off. Gather your personal belongings and go to the basement.

_____ These steps are fairly clear. Please follow them whenever there is a tornado warning. Let me know if you have any questions or need more details.

_____ During last week's tornado warning, it became clear that we need to set up an emergency plan. Here is the plan we should follow during tornado warnings.

C. On a separate piece of paper, write the memo you planned and organized in Exercise C on page 75.

After you write, you need to check what you have written. The two steps below will help you check your work.

Check Your Ideas and Organization. Make sure you used all the ideas in your planning list. Check that the ideas are in the right order. Make sure all the ideas are about the topic. Be sure your topic and purpose come across clearly to readers.

Check Spelling, Punctuation, and Grammar. Check a dictionary to make sure you spelled words correctly. Check the punctuation marks. Did you use periods, question marks, and commas correctly? Then check the **grammar.** Use the rest of this handbook to help you.

When Tiffany Clark checked her writing, she found two problems with her memo. She forgot to give the location of the training. She also used *too* instead of *to* in the last sentence. She wrote the information she forgot. She circled the mistake.

The department will begin using the new computer system in about two weeks.

In order to help everyone learn the new system, two training sessions have been scheduled. Here are the times, dates, and locations of the sessions:

Tuesday, July 27	2 to 4 P.M.	*Include*
Thursday, July 29	9 to 11 A.M.	*place*

The new computer system offers several advantages over the old one. It will let us enter orders more quickly. It will also let us tell customers whether their orders are in stock.

I look forward too seeing you at the training sessions.

Exercises

A. Answer the questions.

1. What two things do you do when you check your writing?

   _____

   _____

2. What should you do to check the spelling of a word?

   _____

   _____

B. Read the ad. Check its ideas, organization, spelling, punctuation, and grammar. Circle the mistakes. Write any information that is missing.

FIFTH ANNIVERSARY SALE!

Thompson's Bakery

Next week we will be celebrating our fifth anniversary. check out these anniversary specials!

Appel Pie *$2.00*
Cinnamin Coffee Cake *$3.50*
Chocolate Cake *$2.75*
Giant Chocolate Chip Cookie *$1.00*

No one else sells baked goods this good and this fresh? So hurry to Thompson's. On tuesday, all customers get a free slice of birthday cake!

C. Check the memo you wrote on page 77 for the following: ideas, organization, spelling, punctuation, and grammar. Circle the things you want to correct. Write down any information you want to add.

Revising, or rewriting to correct problems and mistakes, is the last step in the writing process. When you revise, you fix the problems and mistakes you found when you checked your work. The two steps below will help you revise your writing.

Revise Your Ideas and Organization. Use these tips to correct the mistakes you found when you evaluated your ideas and organization.

- Delete unneeded words or sentences.
- Change the order of sentences and ideas.
- Add missing information.
- Cross off unnecessary information.

Fix Spelling, Punctuation, and Grammar. Correct the mistakes you found when you checked spelling, punctuation, and grammar.

When you revise, you can either retype or rewrite your document. If you wrote on a computer, you can add your corrections to the document and print a new copy.

Here is the final version of Tiffany Clark's memo after she revised it.

MEMORANDUM

TO: Order Processing Department
FROM: Tiffany Clark
SUBJECT: Computer Training
DATE: July 21, 199X

The department will begin using the new computer system in about two weeks.

In order to help everyone learn the new system, two training sessions have been scheduled. Here are the times, dates, and locations of the sessions:

Tuesday, July 27   2 to 4 P.M.   Conference Room A
Thursday, July 29   9 to 11 A.M.   Conference Room B

The new computer system offers several advantages over the old one. It will let us enter orders more quickly. It will also let us tell customers whether their orders are in stock.

I look forward to seeing you at the training sessions.

Tiffany Clark added the places where the sessions will take place and corrected the spelling of the word *to.*

Exercises

A. Answer the questions.

1. What does revising mean?

   _____

2. Name two ways to revise your ideas.

   a. _____

   b. _____

B. Rewrite the ad you evaluated in Exercise B on page 79.

_____

_____

_____

_____

_____

_____

_____

_____

_____

_____

C. On a separate piece of paper, rewrite the memo you wrote on page 77 and evaluated on page 79.

Writing Checklist

Use the following checklist each time you get ready to write. Check off each step as you complete it.

Stage 1 Gathering and Organizing Ideas

☐ Choose your topic.

☐ Decide on your purpose.

☐ Take notes.

☐ Group your ideas.

☐ Choose your ideas.

☐ Put your ideas in order.

Stage 2 Writing

☐ Write the introduction.

☐ Write the body.

☐ Write the conclusion.

Stage 3 Checking

☐ Check your ideas and organization.

☐ Check spelling, punctuation, and grammar.

Stage 4 Revising

☐ Revise your ideas and organization.

☐ Revise spelling, punctuation, and grammar.

Check What You've Learned will give you an idea of how well you've learned the writing skills you'll need to use in the workplace.

Read each question. Circle the letter before the answer.

1. Debbie is filling out an application to work as an admissions clerk in a hospital. Her application form will

   a. include a resume.
   b. give the hospital a chance to see how careful she is in her work.
   c. include a cover letter.

2. Maria is responding to a job ad that she saw in the newspaper. Maria should enclose a resume and a(n)

   a. cover letter.
   b. application.
   c. follow-up letter.

3. Carl fills out a W-4 form in order to

   a. show that he is authorized to work in the United States.
   b. indicate how much of his income should be withheld for taxes.
   c. state whether he wants the employer's health insurance.

4. Theo needs to tell his employees about the company's new policies. Writing a memo means that

   a. all the employees will need to stop working at the same time.
   b. everyone will have a written record of the new policies.
   c. Theo can immediately get feedback from the employees.

5. Donna's performance appraisal is based on

   a. the quality of Donna's work.
   b. the length of time Donna has worked with the company.
   c. Donna's hourly pay.

6. Tamara's customer service letter includes a heading, inside address, body, and closing. What is missing?

   a. the inquiry
   b. the order number
   c. the greeting

7. Brett is completing a personal data sheet. He lists his references. Which of the following could he also include?

   a. a list of all courses taken in high school
   b. volunteer experience at a homeless shelter
   c. a list of resources

8. Luke has typed some names and addresses into the database file. He needs to write the main information of the form letter. What is this information called?

   a. the header
   b. boilerplate
   c. a field

9. Gene's resume has the following: name, address, phone number, education, experience, and skills. He also included references. What is missing from his resume?

   a. the objective
   b. a sample report
   c. performance appraisal

10. Barbara just got home from an interview. She would like to tell the interviewer how much she enjoyed the interview. Barbara should write a

    a. follow-up letter.
    b. personal data sheet.
    c. cover letter.

11. Gwen is writing a sales report about the past six months. In what order might Gwen list her amounts?

    a. alphabetical by month
    b. chronological
    c. alphabetical by customer name

12. Jacob needs to give a detailed account of a sales conference to ten people. Which of the following is *not* an appropriate way to communicate this information?

    a. e-mail
    b. report
    c. memo

13. Howard is proofing his marketing report for a new client. He sees that one of the names is spelled incorrectly. How could Howard quickly correct this error on his computer file?

    a. use a search/find/replace command
    b use a spelling program
    c. use the save as command

Review Chart

This chart will show you what lessons you should review. Reread each question you missed. Then look at the appropriate lesson of the book for help in understanding the correct answer.

Question Check the questions you missed.	Skill The exercise, like the book, focuses on the skills below.	Lesson Review what you learned in this book.
1._____	Filling out an application	2
2._____	Writing a cover letter	4
3._____	Completing a W-4 form	6
4._____	Writing a memo	8
5._____	Completing a performance appraisal	10
6._____	Writing a customer service letter	12
7._____	Creating a personal data sheet	1
8._____	Writing a form letter	11
9._____	Writing a resume	3
10._____	Writing a follow-up letter	5
11._____	Writing a report	13
12._____	Understanding how to use e-mail	9
13._____	Understanding how to use a computer to write	7

adjective: Word that modifies a noun or pronoun only. page 67

adverb: A word that modifies a verb, an adjective, or another adverb. page 67

apostrophe: A punctuation mark used to indicate missing letters in a contraction. It is also used to show ownership. page 59

backing up: Saving a document to have an extra copy. page 30

body: The main part of a document in which a writer often develops and explains ideas. page 76

boilerplate: Information that is the same in each form letter. page 46

chronological: The order in which events happened. page 53

colon: A punctuation mark (:) used after a word that introduces something, such as a list. page 59

comma: A punctuation mark (,) that tells a reader when to pause in a sentence. page 59

conclusion: The last part of a document in which a writer often summarizes or reviews the topic and purpose. page 53

confidential: Something that is private. page 41

consonant: Any letter that is not a vowel. page 69

contraction: A word formed by removing letters from two words and joining the words with an apostrophe in place of the missing letters. page 59

database file: A collection of information usually stored in a computer. page 45

delete: To take out or remove text. page 30

edits: Changes or corrections to text. page 29

fields: Blocks of type contained in a database. page 45

follow-up letter: A business letter that a person writes after an interview. page 19

formal: Proper. page 15

format: The way a document, such as a resume, is set up or organized. page 12

grammar: The rules for using words and structuring sentences. page 78

homonyms: Words that sound alike but have different meanings and spellings. page 70

income: The money a person earns from a job. page 22

independent clauses: Complete thoughts that can stand alone as sentences if punctuated properly. page 61

input: To type information into a computer or word processor. page 29

internal communication: A sharing of information inside a company, such as a memo. page 33

introduction: The beginning section of a piece of writing. It tells what the topic and purpose are. page 75

irregular verb: A verb that does not have a *-d* or *-ed* past tense form. Irregular verbs change form in various ways. Irregular verbs do not follow regular rules. page 65

merge: To join something together, such as two computer files. page 45

misplaced modifier: A modifier placed too far away from the word or phrase it is modifying. page 67

modifier: A word or phrase that describes other words or phrases. page 67

noun: A word that names a person, place, or thing. page 63

order: A purchase. page 49

outline: A summary of the most important points about a subject. page 12

period: A punctuation mark (.) that ends a statement. page 59

plural: The form of a noun that shows there is more than one of something. page 63

policy: A way of doing things. page 33

progress report: A report that states facts and traces developments that have happened over a period of time. page 52

pronouns: Words used in place of nouns. Pronouns do not name specific people, places, or things. page 63

proofread: To check for errors. page 20

question mark: A punctuation mark (?) that ends a question. page 59

rate: To judge how good something is and to assign a score. A rating is a grading or sum of scores. page 40

recommend: To suggest. page 52

references: The names of people who know and like an employee's work. page 12

regular verb: A verb that forms its past tense by adding *-d* or *-ed*. Regular verbs follow regular rules. page 65

reply: To answer. page 37

research: Information a person has studied carefully. Often research includes information learned from books or meetings. page 52

resume: A written outline of a person's background or past experience. page 12

revising: Rewriting to correct problems and mistakes. page 80

run-on: Two or more sentences that are written together without correct punctuation. page 61

save: A command on a word processor or a computer that allows a user to save a document so he or she can look at it again and again. page 30

search/find/replace: The search or find command on a word processor or computer allows a user to find certain words or phrases in text. A user can use the search command with the replace command to substitute one word or phrase for another. page 30

select: To choose. When a person selects text on a computer or word processor screen, he or she highlights text to tell the computer to make a change. page 29

sentence fragment: A group of words that does not state a complete thought. page 61

sequence: In a logical order. page 53

subject-verb agreement: Both the subject and the verb of a sentence agree or match. page 65

survey: A list of questions about a subject. page 52

tense: Shows the time of action of a verb. page 65

topic: The subject you write about. page 52

undo: A command on a word processor or computer that can undo a mistake and bring back text to the way it was before the mistake was made. page 30

verb: A word that expresses action or being. page 65

vowel: One of the letters *a, e, i, o, u,* and sometimes *y.* page 69

withhold: To take out. page 22

word processor: A type of electronic business machine that works like a typewriter but that has many automated features. page 29

Answer Key

For many exercises in this book, several answers are possible. You may want to share your answers with your teacher or another learner.

Check What You Know (pages 1–3)

1. (c)	2. (c)	3. (a)	4. (a)
5. (a)	6. (b)	7. (c)	8. (a)
9. (c)	10. (c)	11. (c)	12. (a)
13. (c)			

Lesson 2: Application Form

Vocabulary Check (page 10)

Answers in order: qualifications, policy, interview, available, salary, notification, authorize, investigate

Comprehension Check (page 10)

1. dental assistant
2. $300/week
3. no
4. Shaw University Hospital
5. She moved to Chicago.
6. It means that she gives the company permission to check out all the facts in her application.

Lesson 3: Resume

Vocabulary Check (page 14)

Answers in order: qualified, background, format, outline, optional

Comprehension Check (page 14)

1. (a)   2. (c)   3. (a)

Lesson 4: Cover Letter and Business Envelope

Vocabulary Check (page 18)

Answers in order: business, formal, body, greeting, envelope

Comprehension Check (page 18)

1. office worker
2. New Century Manufacturers
3. Answers include: worked for two years as a file clerk and telephone receptionist; computer and data entry classes
4. a phone call requesting an interview with him

Lesson 5: Follow-Up Letter

Vocabulary Check (page 21)

Answers in order: follow-up, interviewer, initiative, enthusiasm, proofread

Comprehension Check (page 21)

1. It shows what kind of person you are.
2. It thanks the interviewer for his or her time.
3. Since it is not an application requirement, sending one shows that you do more than is required.
4. If the interviewer asked for more information during the interview, send it.

Lesson 6: Forms: W-4, I-9, and Medical Insurance

Vocabulary Check (page 26)

1. withhold 2. enroll 3. dependent
4. marital status 5. beneficiary
6. Disability

Comprehension Check (page 26)

1. F	2. F	3. F	4. T
5. T	6. F		

Lesson 7: Writing with a Computer

Vocabulary Check (page 31)

Answers: 1. word processor 2. hard copy
3. delete 4. replace 5. spelling checker
6. input 7. select 8. save

Comprehension Check (page 32)

    1. (b)   2. (b)   3. (c)

Lesson 8: Memos

Vocabulary Check (page 35)

    Answers in order: internal, announcements, instructions, policy, update, summary, details, request for action

Comprehension Check (page 35)

    1. F   2. T   3. T   4. F
    5. F   6. T

Lesson 9: E-mail and Phone Messages

Vocabulary Check (page 38)

    Answers in order: e-mail, formatted, transmit, header, reply

Comprehension Check (page 38)

    1. (a)   2. (c)   3. (b)

Lesson 10: Performance Appraisal

Vocabulary Check (page 43)

    1. evaluation 2. volume 3. initiative
    4. confidential

Comprehension Check (page 43)

    1. 1 year
    2. 8
    3. $13/hr.
    4. Answers include: attitude and cooperation, ability to get along with others
    5. He is an excellent employee who consistently exceeds expected levels.

Lesson 11: Form Letters

Vocabulary Check (page 48)

    1. merge 2. database 3. boilerplate
    4. header

Comprehension Check (page 48)

    1. database and word processing

    2. It creates a personalized form letter.
    3. to communicate similar information to a large number of people without retyping every letter
    4. Answers include: name, address, ZIP code, city, state, company, title

Lesson 12: Customer Service Letters

Vocabulary Check (page 51)

    1. inquiry 2. complaint 3. request
    4. resolve

Comprehension Check (page 51)

    1. F   2. F   3. F   4. T
    5. T   6. F

Lesson 13: Reports

Vocabulary Check (page 55)

    Answers in order: research, topic, progress, survey, conclusion

Comprehension Check (page 55)

    1. (a)   2. (b)

Handbook

Capitalization (page 58)

    A. 1. On Monday, Ursula Lawson applied for a job as a junior assistant to Mayor Blake.
      2. She drove down Haynes Road to get to Mayor Blake's office in the Price Building.
      3. One of the mayor's assistants, Mr. Crawford, asked Ursula to fill out an application.
      4. On the application, Ursula was asked if she was a citizen of the United States.
      5. Ursula filled out the application on Monday, July 1, 1997.
    B. Answers in order include: By, Cleveland, From, April, January, Senator Cass, Sacramento, California, One, California, University of Northern California, Ohio

Punctuation (page 60)

A. 1. ?
   2. .
   3. .
B. 1. June 1, 1998
   2. $1,100
   3. South Bend, Indiana
C. 9:00, 5:00, following:
D. 1. Jonathan's 2. Don't, It's 3. shouldn't
   4. She's 5. Tory's 6. It's, mother's
   7. Who's 8. What's

Run-ons and Sentence Fragments (page 62)

A. 1. James, the human resources manager, hired a qualified person to fill the entry-level accounting position. She had experience in accounting.
   2. Her resume listed three previous jobs she held in finance. She worked for Electricus for the past eight years.
   3. Shawn was repairing the engine. The customer called to ask when he could pick up his car.
   4. Shelly opened the flower shop early in the morning for her suppliers. They often arrived before 7:30.
B. 1. F   2. F   3. C   4. F
   5. C   6. F

Nouns (page 64)

A. 1. speeches 2. classes 3. businesses
   4. disks 5. courses 6. buses 7. addresses
   8. taxes
B. 1. Maricela, balance, she, it, bank
   2. end, day, police officer, arrest reports, he, them, his, assistant
   3. Sharon, receipts, day, she, cash, her, register
C. 1. It 2. They 3. They

Verbs (page 66)

A. Answers in order from left to right and top to bottom in the chart: worked; will work; understand; understood; think; will think; had; will have; apply; applied; go; will go; knew; will know; call; will call; sent; will send

B. 1. checked
   2. used
   3. did; began
   4. told
C. 1. will organize 2. pushed 3. drive

Modifiers (page 68)

A. 1. well 2. good 3. quickly, carefully
   4. Slowly 5. easy, beautifully
B. 1. The chef mixed the ingredients for the filling in the blender.
   2. Correct
   3. The painter, wearing overalls, began work on the house.
   4. The department leaders can complete the new project by scheduling meetings in the evenings.
   5. Correct
   6. Walking from her office to the meeting, she said something about the finance department's report.
   7. Jennifer was cleaning out the file cabinet containing over fifty software disks.

Spelling (pages 71–72)

A. for; two; here; see; piece; right
B. 1. stopped, stopping 2. named, naming
   3. worked, working 4. timed, timing
   5. phoned, phoning 6. wrapped, wrapping 7. inputted, inputting
   8. ordered, ordering 9. hired, hiring
C. 1. you're 2. I'll 3. Here's 4. there 5. It's
   6. We're 7. who's 8. He'll 9. We've 10. wait
D. 1. friend 2. Neither 3. taking 4. receive
   5. believe 6. biggest 7. assistant 8. weight
   9. their 10. February 11. appreciate
   12. pieces 13. saving 14. science

The Writing Process (page 75)

A. 4, 2, 3, 6, 5, 1
B. the job I'm applying for 1
   ~~I played in the band~~
   ~~I have two brothers and a sister~~
   when I'm available for an interview 5
   I get along well with people 4
   I play several sports and know a lot about sporting goods 3
   I found the job listing on the Internet 2

(page 77)

    A. 1. (c) 2. (a) 3. (b)

    B. First paragraph: 2; Second paragraph: 3; Third paragraph: 1

(page 79)

    A. 1. check the ideas and organization; check the spelling, punctuation, and grammar

       2. Look up the word in a dictionary.

    B. Circle misspelled words *appel, cinnamin* (correct spelling *apple, cinnamon*). Capitalize the first letter of *check* and *tuesday*. Put a period after *fresh*. Also the ad needs to give the dates of the sale, the address of the store, and the hours it is open.

(page 81)

    A. 1. rewriting to correct problems and mistakes

       2. Answers include: Delete unneeded words or sentences, change the order of sentences and ideas, add missing information, cross off unnecessary information.

Check What You've Learned
(pages 83–85)

1. (b)	2. (a)	3. (b)	4. (b)
5. (a)	6. (c)	7. (b)	8. (b)
9. (a)	10. (a)	11. (b)	12. (a)
13. (a)			

WORKFORCE: BUILDING SUCCESS

COMMUNICATION	0-8172-6517-1
TIME MANAGEMENT	0-8172-6518-X
PERSONAL DEVELOPMENT	0-8172-6519-8
PROBLEM SOLVING	0-8172-6520-1
CUSTOMER SERVICE	0-8172-6521-X
WRITING	0-8172-6522-8
TEACHER'S GUIDE	0-8172-6523-6

STECK-VAUGHN®
COMPANY
ELEMENTARY · SECONDARY · ADULT · LIBRARY

ISBN 0-8172-6522-8

9 780817 265229

P6-CGL-410